blue
rider
press

WE'RE STILL
RIGHT

THEY'RE STILL
WRONG

WE'RE STILL RIGHT

THEY'RE STILL WRONG

The Democrats' Case for 2016

JAMES CARVILLE
WITH RYAN JACOBS

Blue Rider Press • New York

blue
rider
press

An imprint of Penguin Random House LLC
375 Hudson Street
New York, New York 10014

Copyright © 2016 by Gaslight, Inc.
Penguin supports copyright. Copyright fuels creativity, encourages diverse
voices, promotes free speech, and creates a vibrant culture. Thank you
for buying an authorized edition of this book and for complying with
copyright laws by not reproducing, scanning, or distributing any part of it
in any form without permission. You are supporting writers and allowing
Penguin to continue to publish books for every reader.

Blue Rider Press is a registered trademark and its colophon
is a trademark of Penguin Random House LLC

ISBN 9780399576225

Printed in the United States of America
1 3 5 7 9 10 8 6 4 2

Book design by Lauren Kolm

To Bill and Hillary Clinton

CONTENTS

A Letter from the Author *xiii*

Prologue: 1.6 Billion Facts & a Snowball *1*

Introduction: America's Muller Moment *11*

Snake Oil or the Cure? *23*

America Isn't What It Used to Be *83*

Shit Sandwiches *113*

The Anatomy of Bullshit *155*

Interlude: Where We Were Wrong *191*

Trump's Original Sin *199*

I'd Sooner Work for Kim Jong-un *207*

Conclusion: Do Facts Matter Anymore? *213*

Appendix: A Voter Guide for 2016 *223*
Acknowledgments *227*
Notes *229*
Illustration Credits *241*
About the Author *243*

A LETTER FROM THE AUTHOR

Dear Reader,

I'm a guy who likes to traffic in metaphors and analogies. Some pundits use words like "ideologically divisive" or "partisan entrenchment" to describe our politics. But, for me, the tribal nature of American democracy can always be described with more colorful words, phrases like "dogfight" or "pissin' contest" or "pig slaughter"—a *boucherie*, as we say in Louisiana.

Maybe I got this literary nature from my momma, who went door-to-door selling encyclopedias. Maybe it's just the way we Cajuns talk. But whatever the reason, last year, when I thought about the upcoming presidential election, the metaphor I chose was a grand celebration.

I envisioned a party. *A literal Republican party.*

I could see it all, clear and bright. There they were, all

the Republicans in Congress who'd been hoisted to victory in the 2014 midterm landslide.

And there were the Republican governors—all thirty-one of them—standing sentry by the bathroom doors, ready to pounce should a transgender person walk in.

And there were Hannity, Rush, and O'Reilly, surrounded by a bevy of blonde commentators, clinking glasses of a beautiful red punch served by white-gloved girls from the Junior League.

Oh, my friend, it was all so vivid! It was as clear as my crystal scotch glass, and the clearest vision of all was the bright center of the affair. There, huddled around the punch bowl, were the presidential candidates themselves. Not all the "candidates" were there, of course. Not the carnival barkers or the "outsiders." Only the real candidates had been invited. Among them were five governors and four senators, the most promising batch of Republican contenders in a generation, with a collective 193 years of experience in elected office.

What were they doing? you ask. Well, they were laughing of course. They were guffawing their lily-white asses off.

And why not?

At the moment of this particular fiesta, the Republican Party controlled the House, the Senate, and the vast majority of state legislatures and governors' mansions across the country.

Basically, all the GOP needed now was an easy 270 electoral votes on Election Day, and then they'd effectively control the entire government. It would be a Republican paradise, just like the 1950s. The GOP would be able to pollute what they wanted . . . deregulate what they wanted . . . and discriminate against whom they wanted! The only thing standing in their way was the Democratic competition, which happened to be a seventy-four-year-old socialist and a woman under FBI investigation.

So, yes, of course the candidates were laughing—and laughing loudly—as they sipped their punch, a dazzling crimson punch with lime wedges and just the right amount of Veuve Clicquot champagne.

In fact, maybe it was all that celebrating that kept the GOP dull-eyed to the intruder in their midst. Maybe it was the laughter—or the alcohol—that kept everyone from noticing there was an uninvited guest, a person who was just then landing his helicopter outside.

Indeed, someone was crashing this Republican party, but no one knew it until the ballroom doors flew open and in walked a man who promptly strode to the center of the party. He straddled the punch bowl, dropped his pants, and whipped out his member, which, he assured everyone, was very large.

Then Donald Trump pissed right into the punch bowl of the Republican Party.

AS I'M WRITING THIS, I DO NOT KNOW FOR ABSOLUTELY SURE that Trump will be the GOP presidential nominee. It's May now. The Republican National Convention is still three months away, and for all I know, the delegates in Cleveland could give the big prize to Trump or to Speaker of the House Paul Ryan or to the cryogenically frozen head of Walt Disney. Frankly, it does not matter.

Win, lose, or draw in Cleveland, Trump has presided over the death of the Republican Party as we knew it. In a race that seemed like a lock for the leading lights of the GOP, Trump found a rip in the body politic, an edge like one of those perforated lines on a ketchup packet that says, TEAR HERE. Except, in this case, the line divided the GOP's "Establishment" from its base, and Trump tore it away with his tiny stumpy fingers. He ripped the party straight through the gut.

Today we have a Republican Party where voters hate the party leaders, and the party leaders hate the voters. In fact, the magazine *National Review* is the closest thing the GOP has to an official publication, and one of their main contributors, Kevin Williamson, painted Trump supporters as loser drug addicts, writing that "the truth about these dysfunctional, downscale communities is that they deserve to die."

"Donald Trump's speeches make them feel good," he wrote. "So does OxyContin."[1]

Of course, the billion-dollar question of this election cycle has been: Why did this Republican civil war happen?

Why Trump?

Why now?

Well, there are probably a thousand explanations for Trump's hostile takeover of the GOP. There are demographic shifts and economic indicators that help explain it, and I'll get into many of them later on. But sometimes the best explanation is the simplest one: Trump happened because the Republican Party had been so wrong . . . for so long . . . about so many things. That also happens to be a core argument of this book:

Trump succeeded because the Republican Party failed.

For thirty years, Republican politicians—everyone from Reagan, to W. Bush, to Paul Ryan—have shown up in those hardscrabble towns that the *National Review* talked about. They've visited dilapidated bandstands and the union watering holes, places where they don't serve Veuve Clicquot champagne—just dollar beers and a shot. And those politicians have offered the voters the same bargain every time.

That bargain went something like this:

If you allow us to cut taxes for our donors . . . and allow us to slash your Social Security and Medicare benefits . . .

and let us gut any regulation and negotiate any kind of trade deal we want . . . then we'll let you keep your guns. And by the way, all of this will actually be good for you in the long run.

Trust us, they said. *You'll be able to afford more than a dollar beer soon.*

Well, Republican voters did trust them for a long time. They believed that prosperity was just around the corner, and they waited for it . . . and waited for it . . . and waited for it . . . until they could wait no longer.

Think about it. It's 2016. Sixteen percent of the century is over, and not only has the Republican Party failed to deliver on their bargain—their policies have not helped struggling communities—but they've also been wrong about everything else. This is the party that told us that the Bush tax cuts were going to help the middle class, not explode the deficit . . .

THEN they told us that Saddam had weapons of mass destruction . . .

THEN that Iraqis were going to greet us as liberators . . .

THEN that the Bush administration was doing a "heckuva job" during Katrina . . .

THEN that the "fundamentals of the economy were strong" . . .

THEN that Obamacare was going to wreck the economy . . .

THEN that Romney was going to win Ohio and "slip into the presidency" . . .

THEN that we'd have six-dollar gas once Obama got reelected . . . and a crashed stock market . . . and 8 percent unemployment . . .

AND finally, they told us that we were all going to catch Ebola and die.

My God! The only organization with a worse record this millennium has been the Oakland Raiders. At some point, voters were going to wake up. Of course they were going to mutiny like deckhands on a ship captained by idiots. And that point came this year.

Unfortunately, the wake-up call also came in the form of a tangerine with the political leanings of Generalissimo Francisco Franco, otherwise known as Donald J. Trump.

Why Trump?

Why now?

Because the Republican Party has failed, and Trump is

the living, breathing manifestation of that failure. He may have pissed in the GOP's punch bowl, but the truth is, the party was over before the punch was spiked with Trump's pee. It had died long before he came along, and the cause of death wasn't murder but suicide. A long, slow suicide. It was the sum total of twenty years of wrongness.

In a lot of ways, what follows is a chronicle of that wrongness. Consider this book an autopsy of sorts. It's the story of why the Republican Party died, why it should remain dead (especially if Trump is at the helm), and—most important—why the Democratic Party should not follow it to the grave.

Laissez les bon temps roulez!

James Carville
May 1, 2016
New Orleans, Louisiana

P.S. Some chefs like to pair their meals with wine. Well, I'm one author who likes to pair his books with food and drink. It's part of being Cajun, I guess. We can't do anything without thinking about what we're going to eat next. So throughout the book, you're going to find little recipes like this. (I call them *lagniappes*, which is a Cajun word for "a little extra.")

THE REPUBLICAN PARTY'S DAZZLING RED PUNCH: LET'S TOAST TO THE END OF THE GOP

INGREDIENTS

- 12 ounces cranberry juice
- 12 ounces pink lemonade concentrate, frozen
- 6 ounces limeade concentrate, frozen
- 3 bottles Veuve Clicquot champagne
- 1 liter club soda
- 10 limes, quartered for garnish

DIRECTIONS

Combine all ingredients except the limes and stir punch vigorously. Pour in a bowl with ice to keep punch cool. Garnish with lime quarters. Set bowl out of reach of children and orange-faced, tiny-handed partygoers.

WE'RE STILL RIGHT

THEY'RE STILL WRONG

1.6 Billion Facts & a Snowball

According to anyone's political instincts, what I'm about to do is ass-backward stupid.

You don't begin a book in Berkeley, California. Not if you're trying to win converts to the Democratic Party. It's too liberal, too alienating for moderates.

You only begin in Berkeley if you are shilling for Republicans. Then it's an easy case to make. You talk about the college town's unbridled hedonism, a modern-day Sodom. You mention the braless students . . . the hydroponic marijuana farms . . . the flag-burning rallies . . . the classes in pansexual theory. And you punctuate it with a classic "Thanks, Obama."

I get it. Berkeley can be seen as the embarrassing nephew for Democrats like me. Never mind that I grew up in the farthest place from Berkeley. In Louisiana we were so deep in the sticks they had to pipe in sunlight. Still, I can hear my editors saying, "Why not swap out California for Ohio? Why not begin with a midforties factory worker? Or a white mother of 2.5 children? That's the demographic sweet spot. That's what all the presidential candidates do! *Don't begin in Berkeley.*"

Well, tough shit. Here we are anyway.

The truth is: We have to begin in Berkeley because if you want to understand American politics right now, you have to first understand the story of Richard Muller. And Berkeley is where he lives.

Chances are you don't know Richard Muller. You've probably never heard his name. You should not feel bad about this. I've been polling people—columnists, reporters, my students at Tulane, the professors there. Nobody else has heard of Muller either.

This is strange because for a brief moment at the beginning of the decade Muller was the great hope of conservatives, maybe among the most important people in politics. Muller wasn't a politician, though. He was—and is—a scientist, a physics genius at UC Berkeley straight out of central casting. He's got the tweed jacket, and he looks like he goes to the same barber as Einstein.

But there was one way Muller wasn't like your typical scientist: In 2010 he was unconvinced that the Earth was warming. Muller was a climate change "skeptic." He had looked at the data from the United Nations Intergovern-mental Panel on Climate Change—the group that won a Nobel Prize with my old buddy Al Gore—and he'd found it lacking. The weather stations they'd used to measure temperatures were falling apart, and they'd tossed out a lot of the data. Muller wanted to double-check the work, to discover whether climate change was real for himself.

Muller wasn't an ideological guy. In fact, he took pains to be as evenhanded as he could about his project. "We don't have a political agenda," he told me. "All we are trying to do is to reach an objective conclusion about climate."[1]

Nevertheless, it's easy now to see why he became the high-IQ'd darling of the Right. He was among the very few scientists who publically questioned the reality of climate change, and as Muller put it, "People who ignore the science will point to anybody that is on their side."[2]

And so, in early 2010, Muller witnessed one of the strangest phenomena in American politics: a flood of right-wing support into arguably the most liberal square mile in the country. Charles Koch—who, with his brother, had funneled roughly $40 million to groups that denied cli-mate change—wrote Muller's project a six-figure check.[3]

Even the Internet's most popular climate change skep-tic, a guy named Anthony Watts, became Muller's biggest fanboy. Watts had been denying the climate science for years, and he thought Muller's study would bring some intellectual firepower to his cause. Finally, a skeptic like him was leading the project. "When has that *ever* happened in climate science," wrote Watts. Then he made Muller a promise. "I'm prepared to accept whatever result [you] produce," he said, "even if it proves my premise wrong."[4]

There it was. Muller's project was going to crack open the global warming debate. Or call the fight.

Muller got to work. With his daughter, he founded the Berkeley Earth Science Temperature Project and set up headquarters in his house. He assembled a crack squad. The Nobel Prize winner Saul Perlmutter was advising him. So was Art Rosenfeld, who was once the ace student of Enrico Fermi, aka "the father of the nuclear age." These were some smart, smart gentlemen, and for two years, they pored over 1.6 billion data points. They built their models. They ran their numbers. And when they finished, Muller published a summary of his findings in *The Wall Street Journal*, whose editorial board had recently called global warming a "fad-scare."[5]

Now, I have never been invited inside the offices of *The Wall Street Journal*. (I cannot imagine why.) So I don't know if they adhere to the age-old newspaper tradition of drinking no matter the hour. But if they do, I can tell you they weren't popping champagne on the morning of October 11, 2011.

That morning, Muller's findings hit the *Journal*'s opinion page. "There were good reasons for doubt," he wrote, "until now."[6]

The Earth was warming, Muller said. You could not deny the evidence.

At this point, it seems to me that Muller's backers started getting a bit snippy. Charles Koch's foundation released a statement. They pointed out that Muller had only studied air temperatures—not ocean temperatures—and that he hadn't specifically said humans were to blame.[7]

Fortunately, Muller was already tackling that question. He went back to the data. He measured the ocean temperatures. He studied what could be causing the warming. And after six months, he had his answer.

This time, Muller published in *The New York Times*. "Last year," he wrote, "I concluded that global warming was real and that the prior estimates of the rate of warming were correct. I'm now going a step further: Humans are almost entirely the cause."

"Call me," Muller said, "a converted skeptic."[8]

LET'S STOP HERE FOR A SECOND. POUR YOURSELF A MAKER'S Mark on the rocks. (That's what I do when I think about what might have been.) Because you can guess what's coming next for Dr. Muller—Republicans are about to turn on him—but wouldn't it be wonderful if something else happened?

HERE IS RICHARD MULLER. A SMART MAN DOING A GOOD THING. An American thing. He's properly skeptical of what he's told. Listens to his momma. Doesn't believe everything he reads. So he tests it himself. He goes out and gets some backers. This happens to add credibility to his endeavor. After all, if a Koch-funded study says climate change is real, what else is there to debate? And that is exactly what Muller finds. Climate change *is* real. And humans are the cause.

Imagine a country that accepts that. Imagine a Republican Party that accepts that. Imagine Dr. Muller showing up at the White House in his tux. Imagine the president clapping him on the shoulder and hanging the National Medal of Science around his neck. Imagine Senate Republicans are in the East Room, and they're clapping because they're the ones who pushed for Muller to get the award.

By the way, you still got that bourbon? Good. Drink up.

Because that is not what happened to Dr. Richard Muller.

After Muller released his findings, it turns out that Anthony Watts, the influential blogger who promised to accept Muller's conclusion, wasn't prepared to accept it.[9] And while the Kochs did admit global warming is occurring, they didn't see it as a big problem—and still don't.

I spoke to Dr. Muller on the phone not long ago. He's an incredibly diplomatic individual and is the first to say that he's not in the business of telling politicians what to do (although I think our country would be a heckuva lot better if he did). But even Muller admits that there is a group of people, especially those in politics, who just aren't swayed by the evidence.[10]

As I write this, Muller's data has been public for four years, and the GOP hasn't moved on climate change. Hell, they've slid backward. Their presumptive presidential nominee claims that the concept of global warming was "created by and for the Chinese to make U.S. manufacturing non-competitive."[11] Trump believes climate change is a Chinese hoax! Had The Donald been around in the sixteenth century, he'd be saying that the Earth is round was just a theory to help the Ming dynasty sell souvenir globes. Then he'd demand Galileo's execution.

It's not like Muller has been quiet about his study. He went to Washington. He testified before Congress. But it didn't make much of a difference. In 2015, when the Senate took a vote on whether global warming was man-made, every Republican—except three—voted nay.[12]

One of the "nay" votes was from Jim Inhofe. Heard of him? He's a Republican from Oklahoma and the most vocal climate change denier in Washington. He also happens to be chairman of the Senate Committee on the

Environment and Public Works. One winter he went to the Senate chamber to give a speech about why global warming was a hoax and held up his evidence: a clump of snow he'd picked up outside.[13]

Muller had 1.6 billion data points. The Republicans had a goddamn snowball.

He was right. They were wrong. But it didn't matter.

That's why this book is for Dr. Richard Muller. He may not identify as a political guy, but more and more, American politics is starting to identify with his predicament.

I'll tell you why . . .

NO, SENATOR, CLIMATE CHANGE ISN'T A HOAX, AND NEITHER IS THIS FORMULA FOR AN AUTHENTIC NEW ORLEANS SNOWBALL

One of the great joys of moving my girls back to New Orleans was being able to share the Louisiana tradition of Hansen's Sno-Bliz.

Hansen's, which makes fantastic snow-cone-like desserts, is located on Tchoupitoulas Street in New Orleans and has been family-owned since 1939. Hansen's keeps their recipe for the Sno-Bliz syrup a secret, but if you assemble the ingredients below, you might be able to make something close to the real deal.

INGREDIENTS

* 2 cups shaved ice (try the "ice crush" setting on your blender)
* I cup lemonade, limeade, or root beer (these work as syrup substitutes)
* 2 scoops ice cream (any flavor)
* crushed pineapple
* whipped cream
* I maraschino cherry

DIRECTIONS

Place the shaved ice in a cup and drizzle the syrup on top. Then place your ice cream scoops over the ice and top with crushed pineapple, whipped cream, and the cherry.

INTRODUCTION
America's Muller Moment

Twenty years ago—long before the Koch brothers accidentally helped prove global warming—I wrote a rah-rah book defending the concept of an activist government.

It was a book for the moment. In 1996 Newt Gingrich was still the newly installed Speaker of the House. Two years earlier, his "Republican Revolution" had sent more than sixty Democrats in Congress packing. It was a historic defeat. A massive loss. And as my old boss Bill Clinton approached his reelection, the pundits thought he'd lose, too. Nate Silver was still in high school then, so we didn't have the exact odds, but *The New York Times* described his prospects with "a lingering unease."[1]

I had helped Clinton get to the White House in '92, and, God knows, I wanted him to stay there. But I knew he'd be out on his country ass if Democrats went into

Election Day with sweaty palms and cold feet. You see, elections may be won in the center by converting independents, but they are lost by the base. If your base doesn't show up, you lose. First rule of campaigns: *Rally the troops.*

So ahead of the '96 election, I whipped myself into a proper fighting mood and brought together some hungry young Democrats at my place in D.C. For the next couple of months, we drank scotch and wrote a defense of all that's good and holy according to liberal scripture: Medicare, Medicaid, welfare, and Head Start. We stood up for the progressive tax system and the notion that Democrats were better at creating jobs and closing the gap between the very rich and very poor.

Our argument was similar to an old line that Harry Truman had used against the Republicans. "We're right, and they're wrong," he'd said at the 1948 Democratic National Convention. "And I'm going to prove it to you."

We decided to name the book after Harry's quote. We titled it *We're Right, They're Wrong.* It had that happy warrior sentiment. I liked it. It felt right. But not completely.

To be honest, I wasn't sure we'd really done what Harry had. I wasn't sure we *proved* that we were right and they were wrong. We had data to suggest that Democrats did the most good for the most people, but in 1996 we didn't know that. *We're Right, They're Wrong* was more of a political slogan, not a statement of fact. We were just trying to help liberals find their balls, and on that score we were better navigators than Magellan.

The book did its job. It even hit number one on the *New York Times* best-seller list for a moment. (To be fair, our competition included a paperback about the "352 dangers that beset teenage girls," and since abstinence-only education and the Republican assault on Planned Parenthood were not among them, I felt particularly good about taking the top spot.)[2] But the real highlight of 1996 was that President Clinton stayed President Clinton. He won his reelection, and afterward he called me, saying he'd thought the book helped. I replied, "Thanks, boss."

Then the next twenty years happened.

When I dug *We're Right, They're Wrong* out of storage last fall, I barely remembered it. I'd forgotten who was "we" and who was "they." I didn't even recognize the guy on the cover. (It was me, with hair.) But as I thumbed through it, I recognized the arguments, and it was eerie how well they'd held up. I checked the copyright page. *Did we update this?* No. This was stuff we wrote in '96.

- A decade before subprime mortgages sunk the economy, we fought back on the idea that "the market is rational and the government is dumb."
- We talked about the fact that many black

Americans felt "their greatest opportunity was to get harassed by a cop"—and said that America should reckon with this sooner, not later.

- And we wrote that income inequality was a huge problem at a time when Republicans were actually saying a growing gap between rich and poor was good for America.

People have given me all sorts of nicknames. You've heard of the "Ragin' Cajun." Then there's *Saturday Night Live*, which has called me the "king of the snakes," the "crypt keeper," and a guy who looks like a "family of eels raised him as one of their own." I find those hilarious. But until I rediscovered *We're Right, They're Wrong*, I'd always just gone by "James." Now, however, I've broken the cardinal rule of nicknames and given myself one.

Goddamn, I thought, when I first cracked the book again. *I must be Nostradamus.*

I'm serious. If you're a Democrat and you look at how often we've been right since the turn of the century, you'd think we were a bunch of oracles writing our policy papers with a crystal ball. The Republicans may have run a senatorial candidate who was rumored to be a witch (see: O'Donnell, Christine), but it is us Democrats who actually have the supernatural power of clairvoyance.

A couple of pages back, I gave you a list of issues where Democrats had been right and Republicans had been wrong. Here are a few more that we'll cover in this book:

- Benghazi wasn't actually a criminal conspiracy.
- Income inequality isn't a "truly beautiful" thing.
- Illegal immigration isn't actually getting worse.
- Environmental regulations don't really hurt the economy.
- Wall Street reform didn't end up killing the banking industry.

None of this is an accident. The fact that Democrats have bested Republicans on so many issues is not because Democrats are lucky or clairvoyant. And it isn't because I'm actually Nostradamus (although a good number of Republicans wish I lived in another country—and died three hundred years ago).

Instead, Democrats have been right because ours is the superior position, because our brand of progressivism works and the Republicans' brand of conservatism doesn't. We have twenty years of evidence now to back this up.

So over the next two hundred pages, I'm going to do what I promised back in 1996. *I'm going to prove it to you.*

But if you think it's going to be easy, then you didn't pay attention to the story of Richard Muller.

HERE'S WHAT YOU SHOULD UNDERSTAND BEFORE READING THE book: As many problems as the Republicans have, we Democrats have a problem, too. It's the same problem that Muller had. It's not that the evidence isn't on our side—it is. Our problem is that too many people ignore that evidence. The snag in our political system is not that Democrats are right but that it hasn't mattered. At least not as much as it should.

In many ways, Democrats have enjoyed the opposite record of Republicans—we haven't been abysmally wrong about everything—and yet, we're not enjoying the opposite result. If the Republican Party is cracked and shattered, ours should be stronger than ever, right?

But this isn't the case. The GOP routed us in both the 2010 and 2014 midterms, and I'm not positive that November will reveal a different outcome. The 2016 election has the potential to ruin our party just as much as it ruined the fortunes of Marco Rubio, Jeb Bush, and all the other standard-bearers of the GOP. We're at a critical moment.

I know that you hear some version of this apocalyptic messaging every four years. According to the media and the politicians, every election is the "Most Important Election in Recent American History.™"

Here we stand, they say. *If not us, who? If not now, when?*

That is the choice before us.

Prosperity or oblivion!

Live free or die!

Well, most of the time that's a load of crap.

There's a story that I love about an old running back named Duane Thomas. He played for the Dallas Cowboys in the 1970s, and during the hype before the Super Bowl, the media asked him how it felt to be playing in the ultimate game. Duane replied, "If it's the ultimate game, how come they're playing it again next year?"[3]

Duane's point applies to most elections. But not this one.

In my opening letter, I mentioned that Democrats entered this presidential election season in a dangerous position. Well, we're still in that position: If we lose the presidency in 2016, it likely means that we'll fail to win back the House and the Senate, too. It also means that open federal judgeships will largely be populated by Republicans in robes, and the majority of the statehouses will continue to be occupied by Republican governors and legislators. Democrats will be the party of a couple of big states and some cities, a marginal force on the coasts.

You might think that this future is a long shot, but I think of it in a different way. Out of 325 million people in America, just two have a chance to be our next president. And one of them will surely kill our party. His name is Donald Trump.

As I write this, the prediction markets—websites where people bet on politics—give Donald Trump a 41 percent chance of taking the White House.[4] Those may not be great odds for a candidate in a two-person race, but if I gave you a 41 percent chance of getting hit by a bus while crossing the street, you'd surely keep your sweet ass parked on the sidewalk.

So we're in dire straits here, people. This is what the ancient Athenian general Pericles called "a testing time" and what I'm calling "a Muller moment."

Just like Muller, our party has the data on our side—maybe not 1.6 billion points of it, but data nonetheless. We have facts and evidence and a record, a damn good one. And yet, we still could be silenced by a party that has been nothing but a disaster for the country over the past twenty years.

Donald Trump may have pissed in the GOP's punch bowl, but he's still got enough liquid fury in him to piss in the Democrats', too. And that's a drink I'd rather not have to gulp down come November.

YOU MIGHT BE ASKING, "JAMES, HOW ARE WE GONNA GET OUT of this mess?"

Well, I wish I could tell you that Republicans will suddenly have a change of heart and start looking at the evidence. I wish I could say that they'd read this book and see the error of their ways, but I'm a realist. I've been arguing for Democrats for thirty-five years, and I cannot say that I've converted a single Republican soul. I'm a Catholic, but no saint.

So, no, this book is not for the fire-breathers of the GOP. It's not for the Trump sign holders or the folks dressing up like Paul Revere at a Tea Party rally. If you're one of those folks and you are reading this, I assume you're about to rip out this page, wipe, and flush.

Instead, let me be very clear who this book is for and who can help Democrats solve our Muller problem: It's us. It's Democrats. First rule of campaigns: *Rally the troops.*

There's a reason people don't think Democrats are right as often as we are, and that's because Democrats don't think Democrats are right as often as we are. There are a lot of progressives out there who are not unquestioningly partisan, who are thoughtful, who want to believe that the ideas of the other side have merit. And I know they exist because I am one of them. I want to believe that, as a Democrat, I am wrong about something. I want to believe that there are infinite ways to look at an issue and that many are more valid than mine. Hell, I want to see six sides to the Pentagon. It validates that liberal sentiment that everyone is of value, that everyone has something to add.

The problem is—not everyone does.

There was once a *Washington Post* columnist named David Broder who subscribed to this kind of thinking. Broder was the patron saint of centrism, for whom the answer to any political impasse was always in the middle. If Democrats wanted three dollars in spending and Republicans wanted one dollar, Broder said two dollars was right. He camped out in that elusive spot, the common ground.

The issue with Broderian thinking today is that the common ground doesn't exist. On few, if any, issues can the two parties' thinking intersect. The geometry of politics is all screwed up. For example, where is the common ground between a party that believes global warming is real—and a party that believes it's a myth? Is global warming semifictional then? Is it based on a true story?

Here's another one: Where is the common ground between a party that wants fewer guns—and a party that thinks more guns makes us safer?

Or what about the halfway point between a politician of one party who wants to torture the family members of terrorists and a politician of another party that believes this violates international law and American morality?

This. Has. To. End. We must stop entertaining the idea that we can find value in the Republican Party. We can't abide by this weak, Little League notion that everybody gets a trophy and that we should give the other team extra outs because they're clearly struggling. Because, in case you weren't paying attention, they could still beat us, and beat us badly come November. There's a real chance that, in one year's time, the nuclear codes could be in the hands of a spray-tanned egomaniac whose greatest foreign policy experience is having met Miss Bhutan at a beauty pageant.

So now is not the time to be quiet about our differences or our record of achievement. We cannot be polite about what we've done. I know Democrats catch a lot of grief for "liberal smugness," but it's hard not to be smug when you have bested the other party on nearly every issue. We shouldn't let the country lose sight of our record.

After all, politics isn't a cocktail party. Politics is an all-out fight for the future of America, and we can win it on the merits.

We're right. They're wrong. And, finally, I'm going to prove it to you.

Snake Oil or the Cure?

Much like Ronald Reagan and O. J. Simpson, I became famous twice.

The first time you already know about. It was at the age of forty-eight, after spending months running Bill Clinton's fight for the presidency.

The second time was twelve years later.

It was because I spent two hours on a movie set.

In 2004 I made a cameo in *Old School*, a comedy about a fraternity of misfits and fortysomethings. I thought the script was funny, but I never thought my appearance would come to much. Who remembers a cameo? Flash forward to 2016, and people below the age of forty still stop me on the street and bring it up. They yell Will Ferrell's line at me: "THAT'S THE WAY YOU DEBATE."

If you haven't seen the film, I play myself, and the dean

of a university (Jeremy Piven) brings me in as a ringer in a college debate. He wants to make sure the frat guys lose and are kicked out of school. Will Ferrell is my opponent, and as I'm about to answer a question about biotechnology, he butts in. "Have at it, hoss," I tell Will, and he proceeds to nail the answer.

The scene ends with me openmouthed and stammering. "We have no response," I say. "That was perfect."

The movie is fiction in more ways than one, but that moment struck me as the most unrealistic. See, people in politics, me included, never say "We have no response" in a debate. Debates are our Battle of Britain, and we all think we're Winston Churchill. We never give up. We never surrender. If there's any statistic—any fact—that will back us up, you better believe we fire off that sucker like an anti-aircraft gun aimed at the Luftwaffe.

Anyway, for years, I never thought a presidential candidate would experience a "we have no response" moment in a debate. I didn't think life would imitate art—if you can consider my performance in *Old School* "art"—and I certainly never would've advised anyone to repeat my line. But then I watched Carly Fiorina collide with Gerard Baker of *The Wall Street Journal* on the night of November 10, 2015, during the fourth debate of the GOP primaries. That night Baker dropped the most devastating question of the race.

It was a question that not only undermined Fiorina's candidacy but also the candidacies of everyone sharing the debate stage with her.

The question was about the economy, and there was no response. Well, not really.

Here's the backstory: Carly Fiorina was never a real threat to win the GOP nomination in 2016. She was a footnote candidate in a primary campaign full of them. But as the ex-CEO of Hewlett-Packard—albeit one who was unceremoniously fired—she supposedly could speak about the virtues of the Republican Party on the economy.

This issue, I don't need to tell you, is the GOP's major selling point. For nearly eight years—since Marine One carried Dubya away from the South Lawn and the financial crisis—Republicans have been rebranding themselves. They've tried to win back their position as the party of business savvy and economic growth, casting Democrats as the gang who can't read a spreadsheet or run a Mc-Donald's, let alone manage the largest economy in the world.

The effort began during the debate over the stimulus in 2009, at a closed-door meeting led by the archconservative then-congressman Eric Cantor of Virginia. (More on this later.) For now, let's just say the rebrand has worked. The GOP may have had a hiccup with Obama's reelection, but look at the polls since. Over the last four years, the Pew

Research Center has asked Americans which party they trust on the economy eight separate times. And every time except one the American people said, "Republicans."[1]

Today, the GOP is seen as the party of entrepreneurs and garage inventors and Subway sandwich franchisees, of *Shark Tank* sharks and Harvard Business School deans. In the American mind, GOP = $$$. As for Democrats, we just equal ☹ ☹ ☹. (My kids taught me how to do that.)

This is the notion that Gerard Baker set out to question. *Are Republicans really the party of economic growth?* He wanted to see if Fiorina actually had any evidence to support that brand, specifically on the issue of jobs.

Baker began with some stats challenging the assumption: "In seven years under President Obama, the U.S. has added an average of 107,000 jobs per month. Under President Clinton, the economy added 240,000 jobs a month. Under George W. Bush, it was only 13,000."

Then he unleashed the flamethrower: *"How are you going to respond to the claim that Democratic presidents are better at creating jobs than Republican presidents?"*

Let me pause here to point out that Gerard Baker isn't some token Democrat on the *Journal*'s editorial staff. The man is the editor in chief of the most significant publication of conservative thought. Carly couldn't accuse him of partisanship.

Here is Carly Fiorina's response, unaltered and un-abridged:

> *Well, first of all, I must say as I think about that question, I think about a woman I met the other day. I would guess she was forty years old. She had several children. And she said to me, "You know, Carly, I go to bed every night afraid for my children's future." And that really struck me. This is America. A mother is going to bed afraid for her children's future.*
>
> *And the reason she's afraid for her children's future is because we've had problems for a long time. Yes, problems have gotten much worse under Democrats. But the truth is, this government has been growing bigger and bigger, more corrupt, less effective, crushing the engine of economic growth for a very long time.*
>
> *This isn't about just replacing a Democrat with a Republican now. It's about actually challenging the status quo of big government.*
>
> *Big government has created a big business called politics. And there are lots of people invested in the status quo of that big business called politics. Specifically, we need actually to do five things to really get this economy going again. We need to go to zero-based budgeting so we know where every dollar is*

being spent, we can challenge any dollar, cut any dollar, move any dollar.

We need to actually reform the tax code. Go to a three-page tax code. Yes, there are plans that would reform our tax code to three pages. In addition to rolling back what President Obama has done, we need to do a top-to-bottom review of every single regulation on the books. That hasn't been done in fifty years. We need to pass the REINS Act so Congress is in charge of regulation, not nameless, faceless bureaucrats accountable to no one. We've become a nation of rules, not a nation of laws.

And, finally, we actually, yes, have to hold government officials accountable for their performance. All this has to be done, and the citizens of this nation must help a President Fiorina get it done.

We must take our government back.[2]

Did you get through all of that? No? Well, spoiler alert: Carly never got close to answering the question. She never explained why Democrats were bad job creators or why the premise of Baker's question was wrong.

Instead, she began, as most Republicans do when they don't have a shred of evidence, with a random story that barely qualifies as an anecdote, something about a woman of indeterminate age with vague worries about the futures of an uncertain number of children. It was like a political stump speech Mad Libs—and she forgot to fill in the blanks.

CARVILLE'S FIRST RULE OF ECONOMICS

If you hear a politician answer a question about the economy with a random story, stop listening.

Anecdotal evidence is an oxymoron. The people who rely on it are just morons.

The day after the debate, Carly was panned for her performance; I think I may have grabbed some marshmallows and joined in the roasting. But truth be told, Fiorina shouldn't feel bad for botching the defense of the GOP's record on job creation—nor should her team. They had an impossible task. There was no briefing memo hidden somewhere with the perfect comeback. A comeback didn't exist to Baker's question because it wasn't really a question at all. It was a statement of fact: Republicans don't have any evidence to say they have been better at creating jobs.

The data actually skew the opposite way. Bill Clinton once lit up the 2012 Democratic National Convention by tallying up the "jobs score." Since the Kennedy administration, Democrats and Republicans have occupied the White House for twenty-eight years apiece. Under Democrats, *twice* the number of jobs have been created, including eight million under Obama, he of the "job-killing policies."[3] We aren't just ahead in the "jobs score," we're running it up.

And it's not just jobs . . .

I defy you to find a single major economic indicator that says Republicans are better at handling the economy. Go to the National Archives. Go to the Department of Commerce. Hell, go to the Republican National Committee and look through their e-mails. (See how they like having the tables turned.) You will come back empty-handed, without the data you were looking for. I know this because smarter men than I have searched and failed.

Let me introduce Mark Watson and Alan Blinder, economists from a little-known college called Princeton University.

I've met Blinder before. He's an absolute gentleman and a scholar, the kind of professor you'd meet on your kid's campus, and think, *That must be why I'm hemorrhaging tuition money.* His brain is more valuable to the school than the football team.

Blinder and Watson wanted to study what they called the "unexplored continent of economics."

As they put it, "Everyone knows the economy influences elections, but do elections influence the economy?"

To answer that question, they analyzed sixty-four years' worth of data, from Truman's second term until the end of Obama's first, and when the results came back, they didn't need their PhDs to read them. The data were clear-cut. Other than some very close numbers regarding inflation, every economic indicator was better—productivity, wages, stock market indexes, the pace of the unemployment rate's decline—when one party controlled the White House.

That party was the Democratic Party.

One number stood out in particular to Blinder and Watson: the rate of economic growth.

Over the last six decades, our gross domestic product has risen at an average annual pace of 3.33 percent. But Blinder and Watson found that GDP growth was almost 25 percent slower when Republicans occupied the Oval Office and almost 30 percent *faster* when Democrats did. The gap was "startling," according to the professors, and "there were no exceptions."[4] Had we grown consistently at that Democratic growth rate since 1952, where the study began, our economy would now be the size of two American economies . . . plus a China. On the other hand, had we grown at the aver-

AVERAGE ANNUALIZED GDP GROWTH, BY TERM

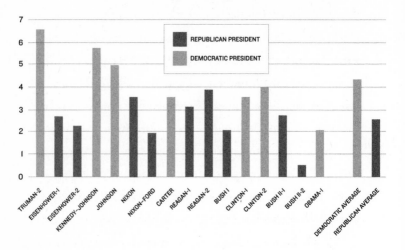

age rate under Republican presidents—2.45 percent—our economy would be the same size as if we'd wiped out every state and city on the Eastern Seaboard, from Washington, D.C., up to New York.[5]

Blinder had once been vice chairman of the Federal Reserve under Clinton, but he didn't seem to find joy in the partisan split in these numbers. He was a Broderian to the core, looking for holes in his work to prove that things were more equal. They weren't. He looked to see if Democrats had just inherited better economies from Republicans. Clinton owed his success to Reagan, right? No. That wasn't the case, Blinder found. Or, he thought, maybe the party that controlled Congress caused the gap, not the presidency? Actually, Blinder and Watson found that the presidency was indeed the best predictor, and growth was best when Democrats held both branches and worse under divided government. Blinder and Watson even checked if minor details like a president's age or height might explain the partisan split. Again, no such luck.[6]

"There is a systematic and large gap," they wrote, "between the U.S. economy's macroeconomic performance when a Democrat is President of the United States versus when a Republican is."[7]

Which brings us back to the question Gerard Baker asked Carly Fiorina. If someone ever asks you to give one piece of evidence proving that Republicans are better on the economy—and that Democrats are worse—just remember that two PhDs from Princeton have tried before you. And they have failed.

So the correct answer to Gerard Baker's question is . . . well, what did I say to Will Ferrell again?

"We have no response. That was perfect."

OBAMA POST-2012: YOUR BALLOT OR YOUR JOB!

Blinder and Watson published their study too early to include an analysis of the economy during Obama's second term, but had they included that data, Democrats would've still maintained their advantage. The year after Obama's reelection—2013—U.S. GDP grew at an annual clip of 1.5 percent. But that rate has climbed to 2.4 percent over the past two years, which is still slow for most Democratic presidents, but not for a commander in chief from the GOP.[8]

GDP-wise, Obama is close to your average Republican!

I prefer, however, to look at Obama's second term through the eyes of one very special job creator: David Siegel, the billionaire founder of the timeshare giant Westgate Resorts.

Lately, Siegel has come under public scrutiny for two reasons.

I. A popular documentary that chronicled his noble quest to build the largest private home in the United States, a tasteful replica of Louis XIV's palace at Versailles.

2. An e-mail he wrote to everyone at his company in 2012.

On the eve of the 2012 election, Siegel sent out a warning to his 12,000 employees: If Obama was reelected and taxes were raised, he would have to fire people. "The economy doesn't currently pose a threat to your job," Siegel wrote. "What does threaten your job however, is another 4 years of the same Presidential administration."[9]

It's been almost four years since Obama trounced Romney—and three years since the Bush tax cuts expired for the wealthy. Shall we check in with Siegel and his employees to hear their tales of misery and woe?

In 2015 I heard Siegel sent his employees another note, but to my surprise, it was not a pink slip. Instead, Siegel told thousands of his workers that they weren't being fired—they were getting raises.

"We're experiencing the best year in our history," he said. "And I wanted to do something to show my gratitude for the employees who make that possible."[10]

No word yet whether Siegel has expressed his gratitude to the president.

THIS IS A CHAPTER ABOUT THE ECONOMY.

Republicans laying claim to being economic saviors is like Democrats laying claim to antiabortion activism or the abolition of Social Security. Our record says the complete opposite. (Thank God.)

The Republican brand is bullshit. You've smelled it by now.

But you might still have questions. *James,* you might be thinking, *the economy is a big and complex thing. The way our government shapes it is even more confusing and unstudied. The Republicans may have a bad track record, but who's to say they won't be better going forward? Or who's to say Democrats will be any better?*

Fair point, and I concede it. After all, Blinder and Watson didn't completely explain *why* the Kennedys, Carters, and Clintons saw faster growth than the Nixons, Reagans, and the Bushes. Just that they did. And that there had to be some reason behind it.

So how do we figure out what that reason is? How do we determine, once and for all, who is the best party to build the American economy and why?

Well, we'd have to use an unimpeachable standard. We couldn't have the GOP accusing us of rigging the game.

If only there was a brilliant economist out there who had such a standard. Of course, this economist would have to be a conservative, too . . . and not just any conservative, but one who actually served under a Republican president . . . and not just any Republican president . . . not a Ford or a Nixon, who may have been more lefty in their fiscal ways . . . but a real conservative president.

Ladies and gentlemen, I give to you Dr. Gregory Mankiw of Harvard University and formerly of George W. Bush's Council of Economic Advisors.

Mankiw says he'd judge the parties on the economy like he'd judge a doctor: "Consider how you would assess a physician whom you could observe treating only a single patient. A terrible way to judge the doctor is by whether the patient lives or dies. After all, even the best physicians have patients who die when their illnesses are severe. And given the natural restorative powers of the human body, even a quack can have a patient who returns to good health.

"The best way to evaluate a physician," Mankiw says, "is to determine whether state-of-the-art medical practices are followed. A doctor who prescribes the right antibiotics gets high marks, while one who prescribes snake oil gets a failing grade."

In other words, look at the policies, not just the outcomes.

I am not opposed to this idea. After all, I hail from Louisiana, perhaps the last place that actually has snake-oil salesmen. So not only do I enjoy your metaphor, Dr. Mankiw, I accept your challenge. Let's look at the policies and give them the Mankiw test.[11]

Let's see who's got the cure . . . and who's selling snake oil.

TAX CUTS: A FIFTH-ROUND KNOCKOUT OF SUPPLY-SIDE ECONOMICS

Talk to a Democrat about tax policy, and you'll either cure his insomnia or get a response with more "but"s than an ashtray at a strip joint in the South.

Democrats don't like taxes—nobody does—*but* we also believe they're the price we pay for civilization . . . *but* right now we also believe that certain tax rates should be lower because the middle class is shouldering too much of the burden . . . *but* we also believe that the country needs to pay for things—roads, schools, health care—and that the wealthy can afford higher rates to help carry those costs. In other words, we aren't dogmatic about this stuff. We have some ifs, ands, and buts about it.

The same is not true of Republicans. Ask a Republican about tax policy, and he will preach to you as if the end is nigh and the Great Beast slouches toward Bethlehem. He will say that tax cuts—only tax cuts, never tax hikes—lead to economic salvation. In fact, in the long-running debate of whether Jesus Christ would vote Republican—a debate that has no significance unless the Second Coming happens in Ohio—I'm surprised that Luke 19:8 doesn't get more attention. It's the story of how Jesus convinced the tax collector to give back half of what he owned. (Jesus essentially implemented Israel's first tax cut!)

Indeed, for Republicans, this is an article of faith, that lowering tax rates, particularly tax rates on the very wealthy, creates economic growth—and that raising them creates utter economic collapse.

The idea didn't just appear out of the blue. It originates with a guy named Arthur Laffer, a very nice economist who was massively wrong about everything. In 1971 Laffer briefly became the laughingstock of the economics community after suggesting that the GDP was skyrocketing and that no one except for him had detected it. He was wrong, but like any good Republican, he wasn't afraid to be wrong again. A few years after his embarrassing prediction, Laffer met with Ford's chief of staff—his name was Dick Cheney—and Laffer shared his new theory on taxes, which he expressed as a parabola—a bell curve—on a cocktail napkin.

It turned out to be the most expensive napkin in history.

The basic idea behind tax rates is that when they increase, the amount of money that the U.S. Treasury collects increases as well. But the Laffer Curve contended that at some point this relationship reverses. The tax rate for the wealthy can become so high, so burdensome, that those very wealthy and intelligent job creators become less motivated to open businesses and invent new things, which means that tax revenue goes down—and, more important, that the economy shrinks.[12]

This is the foundation of supply-side economics, and it may sound reasonable enough, except that Laffer's idea had a fatal flaw: He never figured out where that tipping point was, whether the tax rate would be too burdensome at 1 percent or 99 percent—or anywhere in between.

In 1974 Laffer could've guessed that the tipping point would be ridiculously high based on recent history. During the Eisenhower years, the highest earners paid an income tax of 91 percent, and those were still the economy's best years of the century.[13] He might have suspected that taxpayers would have to get just pennies back on their dollar before we hit the downslope of the Laffer Curve.

But that's not what happened. Since the day Laffer scribbled his parabola on a napkin, three generations of Republicans have professed their fidelity to his brand of economics, including this year's crop of presidential candidates. The highest tax bracket has fluctuated between 28 and 40 percent for the past thirty years—a far cry from the Eisenhower days—and yet, Republicans always claim we're just one small tax increase away from economic collapse and one small tax cut away from Reagan returning to life, galloping across America on his horse with a cloud of jobs and wealth trailing behind him. *Wellll, there he goes agggaaaiin . . .*[14]

The one benefit, however, to seeing supply-side economics in action for thirty years is this: We aren't just looking at a napkin anymore. We have evidence to see if this theory works, which begs the question, Does it?

The answer: Only if your mind can twist in so many loops and curlicues that it could be employed by a circus freak show. Otherwise, it doesn't make a lick of sense.

Let's start with Reagan, the first disciple of Laffer to make it to the White House. Between 1981 and 1988, Reagan lowered taxes on the wealthy dramatically, dropping the highest tax bracket from 70 to 28 percent, and I'll admit the economy did better for a couple of years.[15] You could attribute that upturn to a number of things, including the fact that the business cycle goes through natural ebbs and flows, but for the sake of argument, let's say it was Reagan's tax cuts. According to Laffer's theory, if lowering taxes on the wealthy helped the economy, then raising taxes should hurt the economy, right? If there's a yin, there must be a yang? But this didn't happen when both George H. W. Bush and Bill Clinton increased the tax rate. Instead, we witnessed the biggest economic boom in fifty years.[16]

At this point, the only way Laffer's theory holds up is if

the Clinton years were just a fluke, if the economic boom occurred despite the tax increases and would've been even bigger without those tax increases. This is what conservatives believed when George W. Bush came into office after Clinton and promised to lower taxes. Republicans expected the Bush years to put the Clinton years to shame. A big conservative think tank, the Heritage Foundation, predicted that the Bush tax cuts would juice the economy enough to pay off our entire $3.1 trillion national debt by the end of the decade.[17] Unfortunately, most Americans in 2010 were too busy on the phone with the mortgage company to fact-check the Heritage Foundation on that prediction.

And if you still want to believe in Laffer after the Great Recession, it requires some real mental jujitsu. Because when Obama ran for reelection in 2012, he promised to let the Bush tax cuts expire for the wealthiest Americans and let rates rise back to Clinton's levels. According to the Republican Party, including their nominee for president, this should've tanked the economy. Mitt Romney said tax increases on the wealthy would be a "gut punch to the middle class."[18] Instead, we've witnessed the creation of more than six million private-sector jobs since 2012, and CEOs who said they'd have to fire employees ended up handing out raises instead of pink slips (see: Siegel, David).[19]

Here's the bottom line: After thirty years of "testing" supply-side economics, there's simply no correlation between tax cuts for wealthy Americans and economic growth. There's even less evidence that raising top rates hurts the economy.

The Laffer Curve isn't a worthwhile economic theory. Hell, it isn't even worth the napkin it was written on.

IF THIS WERE A BOXING MATCH, I COULD END THE BOUT RIGHT here, right now. We've had four separate rounds to test supply-side economics—there was Reagan, then H. W. Bush and Clinton, then W. Bush, then Obama—and the last three of those rounds were no contest. If I were a responsible referee, I would call the fight. But then again, I am not a responsible referee. I can't resist some blood on the canvas.

So let's head to a fifth and final round, the knockout round for supply-siders. Because this example lands a powerful haymaker on the last argument they make.

In the brief history of supply-side economics I just recounted, there's always one big problem for the disciples of Laffer: Their claim is that if tax cuts don't appear to work, then there must be some external corrupting influence. For example, they say that Reagan's tax cuts were really responsible for the Clinton boom and that the Gipper would've received even more credit had he been in office for three or four terms. Or they say that George W. Bush's tax cuts really did work, but the economy crashed because Bill Clinton let people buy homes at subprime rates. (Somehow the blame always finds its way back to poor black people.)

Supply-siders believe that if Laffer's theory was tested in a pristine, hermetically sealed economic environment without external factors or influences we'd see its merits. Of course, that kind of environment is practically impossible to create.

But goddamn if Sam Brownback, governor of the deep red state of Kansas, didn't try.

Never in American history has one theory of economics been so fully embraced, so purely tested, as supply-side economics recently was in Kansas.

In 2012 Governor Sam Brownback brought in a "special economic advisor" and began what he called the "march to zero"—that is, the march to zero income taxes. Brownback wanted to eliminate these taxes, which paid for 40 percent of the state's budget, and replace them with modest consumption taxes.[20] His opening gambit was to give all farms and small businesses a complete tax exemption.

"We'll have a real live experiment," Brownback said, and he didn't set expectations low.[21] In a separate op-ed, Brownback wrote that the tax cuts would "pave the way to the creation of tens of thousands of new jobs, bring tens of thousands of people to Kansas, and help make our state the best place in America to start and grow a small business."

"Our new pro-growth tax policy will be like a shot of adrenaline into the heart of the Kansas economy."[22]

It's been four years since Brownback made his "shot of adrenaline" comment, but ask most Kansans and they'll say that the shot felt less like adrenaline and more like a horse tranquilizer straight to the jugular.

After Brownback began his historic "march to zero," the state economy did not take off like a rocket—unless the rocket we're talking about happened to explode on the launch pad and kill everyone inside. Kansas's economy became a disaster zone. By 2015 the state had fallen 18,000 jobs short of the number Brownback had predicted,[23] and its job growth logged far behind neighboring states.[24]

Even worse, Brownback's tax cuts left Kansas in a deep, deep budget hole. Within three years, he had turned the state's $500 million surplus into a $250 million deficit,[25] a reversal of fortunes so disastrous that even Republican legislators were begging Brownback to raise taxes. There was simply no other way for the state to pay its bills. In fact, Brownback himself was so desperate for revenue that at one point right after Tax Day, he sent extra staff down to the mailroom of the state's treasury office. He wanted to make sure they hadn't missed a tax-return envelope filled with a particularly big check. They hadn't.

When the big check never materialized, Brownback and his allies decided to close the budget hole through a combination of small tax increases and huge cuts to education. The cuts were so drastic, in fact, that teachers started "fleeing across the border," looking for work in Missouri.

In a feat of collective stupidity, the state of Kansas re-elected Brownback. But despite that victory, Brownback seems to recognize that his supply-side experiment failed. When the media caught up with him and asked how the "experiment" turned out, Brownback replied, "I shouldn't have used that word."[26]

In fact, the only person who seems to fully stand by the Kansas experiment is that "special advisor" Brownback had initially consulted.[27] Not long after ending a call with Brownback, where he promised the panicked governor that economic growth was just around the corner, that advisor spoke with a reporter. "Kansas is doing fine," the advisor said.[28]

Would you like to know this guy's name? It's Arthur Laffer.

WHEN IT COMES TO TAX CUTS, IT'S PRETTY EASY TO SEE WHO'S selling the medicine and who's selling the snake oil. Here's how the parties score on the Mankiw test:

DEMOCRATIC Rx:

HIGHER TAXES ON THE WEALTHY TO PAY FOR ESSENTIAL PUBLIC GOODS

TAKE: SPARINGLY, AND ONLY AFTER CONSULTING THE AMERICAN PEOPLE.

SIDE EFFECTS: FEW, IF ANY. PATIENTS MIGHT EXPERIENCE HIGHER INTELLIGENCE AND INCREASED LONGEVITY DUE TO THE ABILITY TO PAY FOR BETTER PUBLIC EDUCATION AND HEALTH CARE.

KEY INGREDIENTS: THIRTY YEARS OF EVIDENCE THAT THIS WORKS.

 REPUBLICAN Rx:

SUPPLY-SIDE ECONOMICS (TAX CUTS FOR THE WEALTHY)

TAKE: ALL THE TIME. YOU CAN'T OVERDOSE!

SIDE EFFECTS: SWELLING OF DEFICITS, RAMPANT DELUSIONS INCLUDING VISIONS OF AN ECONOMIC BOOM JUST AROUND THE CORNER.

KEY INGREDIENTS: SNAKE OIL (PROBABLY STILL LACED WITH SOME OF THE VENOM).

SOCIALLY LIBERAL, FISCALLY CONSERVATIVE: THE "I'M WITH STUPID" T-SHIRT OF POLITICS

Back in the '90s, when I published the first version of this book, the novelty T-shirt industry was booming. (Thank God for the march of progress.) Among the best sellers were shirts that read SH*T HAPPENS or had clip art of a smiley face.

The shirt I remember best, though, was one that read I'M WITH STUPID. It was the height of irony: The wearer was implying that the guy standing next to him, his buddy, was stupid, but really, he was the one dressed like an idiot.

I'm not sure if people buy those shirts anymore, but plenty of people in politics are still getting the same message across by saying, "I'm socially liberal but fiscally conservative."

I'm sure you've heard the phrase before, maybe at a cocktail party or a suburban barbecue during an election year. The person means to tell you that their political ideology mixes liberal humanity with conservative frugality, that they're the best of both parties!

They aren't.

"Socially liberal, fiscally conservative" is the I'M

WITH STUPID T-shirt of American politics, and here's why: When people self-identify as "socially liberal, fiscally conservative," they're essentially saying three things:

1. I don't have a problem with gay people. The gays are my friends! (*Well, good for you! Congratulations on not being a bigot. Your momma must be proud.*)

2. But I believe that we need lower taxes and lower deficits. We need a government that spends within its means!

3. I probably also vote Republican. (The polling on this isn't great, but the Pew Research Company did a study of people they called "business conservatives"—i.e., voters who were economically conservative but much more liberal or moderate on social issues. Pew found that 88 percent of those people voted Republican in 2014.)[29]

These folks face an embarrassing problem then, because the Republican presidents have run up the country's debt at much higher rates than their Democratic counterparts. And Donald Trump's plan would put the country deeper in debt than ever before. Trump's tax-cut plan would cost $9.5 trillion, which, according to the head of the Center for a Responsible Federal Budget, is "not even in the universe of realistic."[30]

Bottom line: Most "socially liberal, fiscally conservative" folks look more idiotic than your basic conservatives. They aren't just choosing a party they find morally wrong on issues like same-sex marriage and abortion; they're also picking a party that's produced the exact economic record they detest.

Socially liberal, fiscally conservative is the "I'm with stupid" of American politics.

I may just trademark that and make some T-shirts.

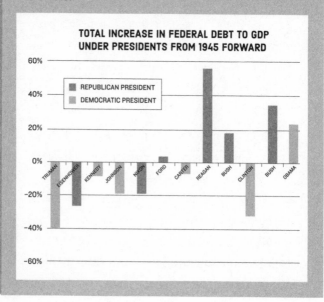

TOTAL INCREASE IN FEDERAL DEBT TO GDP UNDER PRESIDENTS FROM 1945 FORWARD

THE S*!@#%$: WAIT . . . DID THE STIMULUS ACTUALLY WORK?!

According to the late comedian George Carlin, there are seven words I cannot say on television (although this hasn't stopped me from trying). Beyond that, I do not censor myself very much, which is just one of the many reasons I was not employed as a spokesperson in the Obama administration.

Indeed, had anyone been deranged enough to offer me that job, I would've had to add an *eighth* word to my list of banned utterances. That's because the White House also had a word no one was allowed to say. It wasn't similar to any of Carlin's seven vulgarities. This was the administration that employed the foul-mouthed Rahm Emanuel, after all. The banned word was something else.

The word was "stimulus." Or as the White House censors might spell it, "S*!@#%$."

The stimulus, of course, was the $787 billion, 1,073-page, bone-in porterhouse of a spending bill that President Obama signed soon after taking office in 2009. Its aim was to reverse the economy's death spiral at a time when the country was losing 700,000 jobs a month, and its passage was greeted by the president and his team with great fanfare and joy. For the administration, it was the moment in the movie when the surgeon stops the bleeding . . . or when the captain steadies the ship . . . or when Bruce Willis blows up the asteroid. The bill, the president's team said, would be the firewall that kept the Great Recession from becoming greater. It would hold the unemployment rate below 8 percent, they said.

Within a year, however, no Democrat was talking about the stimulus—at least not willingly. When Obama's reelection campaign ramped up, there were no barn-burning speeches celebrating the bill and few MSNBC pundits defending it as an example of what government does right. If cabinet secretaries wanted to talk about the stimulus in their speeches—and very few did—the speechwriters had to use the bill's official name, the American Recovery and Reinvestment Act, because no one knew what that was.[31]

Why did Democrats try to forget about the stimulus? Well, why does anyone try to forget anything . . .

Because they're embarrassed.

The stimulus bill, passed in March of 2009, promised no higher than 8 percent unemployment, but by October, the unemployment rate had crept above 10 percent. By Christmas, polls showed that there were more Americans who believed that Elvis was still alive than those who believed the stimulus created any jobs.[32]

Republicans were calling the stimulus "Porkulus" and a "boondoggle" before the ink was dry on the legislation. But after the 8 percent threshold was passed, they smelled even more blood in the water—and kept up the attack. Five years after the stimulus became law, John Boehner, the then Speaker of the House, was still channeling "millions of families" who were asking, "Where are the jobs?"[33]

That's still the stimulus legacy today: a jobless jobs bill, a twelve-figure boondoggle, the eighth word Democrats can't say on TV. And if you think anything about the stimulus, you probably think it was a massive waste of money.

But was it?

HERE'S THE TRUTH: THE ABOVE NARRATIVE—THE STORY ABOUT the failed stimulus, which Republicans tell and Democrats hang their heads and accept—is utter bullshit.

When it comes to the stimulus, and government spending more broadly, Democrats need to find their goddamn backbone. Not only should we be unafraid to mention the stimulus on television, Republicans should be afraid when Democrats do mention the stimulus on television. Or anywhere.

Other than health care reform, the stimulus is undoubtedly the most misunderstood piece of legislation from the

Obama years. It's also the most underrated and the one where the Republicans had the most preposterous alternative.

Let's go back to the beginning.

The stimulus bill may have been written in a frenzy during the darkest days of the financial crisis, but the idea for the legislation stretches back ninety years, back to when I was still a zygote in Louisiana and a guy named John Maynard Keynes was inventing macroeconomics somewhere in England.

If Arthur Laffer was the intellectual forefather of Republican economics, then Democrats can trace their economic philosophy back to Keynes. He was the economist most responsible for FDR's New Deal, and he believed that in times of great economic distress the government could—and should—step in to spend money the public couldn't.

Republicans may have focused their attacks on the stimulus's more trivial-sounding expenditures—paying for new sod on the National Mall, for example—but what conservatives were really criticizing was Keynes's ninety-year-old idea itself. Keynes had argued that you could juice the economy by paying for work. It didn't matter whether the job sounded trivial; theoretically, you could hire a day shift of workers to dig holes and a night shift to fill them back up. That would still help the economy!

Obama's stimulus didn't fund work that ridiculous.

Not even close. Even the "sod on the Mall" was part of a $200 million project to revitalize America's capital and keep the Jefferson Memorial from sliding into the Tidal Basin.[34] This was necessary work. I, for one, would not like to be part of the generation that drowned the author of the Declaration of Independence.

Nevertheless, in the way Kansas became a flash point for supply-side economics, the stimulus became a modern test of Keynesianism, albeit with one small difference. The difference was: Unlike supply-side economics, experts overwhelmingly believe Keynesian economics works. Laffer is the anti-Keynes. Keynes is the anti-Laffer. His theories were effective not just in FDR's time but in Obama's, too.

Eight years after the stimulus, economists have given their verdict. From the nonpartisan Congressional Budget Office to Goldman Sachs (not exactly a bastion of liberalism), all agree: The stimulus prevented the Great Recession from becoming a second Great Depression, an economic crap storm the likes of which none of us, unless you're well over eighty years old, has ever seen.

What did the stimulus do specifically to help the economy? Well, our friend Alan Blinder (of Princeton) and Mark Zandi, who was an economic advisor to John McCain, paint a picture of an America without the stimulus—and that picture is a hellscape:

- Without the stimulus, the budget deficit would have doubled from 10 percent of GDP to 20 percent. (That's huge!)

- Our economy would have shrunk at more than three times the rate—not by 4 percent, but by 14 percent. Today we'd still feel the effects, with an economy that possessed 800 billion fewer dollars in wealth.

- We'd be living in a country without hundreds of new bridges, enough newly paved highway to stretch around the world, and, yes, new grass on the National Mall.[35] (The money from the stimulus went somewhere, and a good chunk went under our feet, including to the I-10 highway in my hometown of New Orleans that had been ripped apart during Hurricane Katrina and needed repairing.)[36]

I should also mention one other small thing: THE STIMULUS CREATED JOBS! A HELL OF A LOT OF JOBS!

If he could, I'm sure the president would take back the Infamous Prediction of 2009, the promise that the stimulus would keep us under 8 percent unemployment. The idea originated in a chart midway through a report published by the president's economists. A gaffe in a footnote.

But Obama's economists were more correct than they were given credit for. They didn't overestimate how many jobs the stimulus would create. Instead, they underestimated the depth of the hole we were in. This is understandable because analyzing economic data is sort of like watching *Game of Thrones* in Russia: You don't get to see tonight's episode until next month. When Obama's economists first made the Infamous Prediction of 2009, no one was aware of new and disastrous data being collected at that moment from Europe and Japan. The crisis was worse than anyone had imagined.[37]

In any case, the stimulus made a horrible job situation better. The vast majority of experts say so. (See the chart on the following page.)

Blinder and Zandi actually have numbers on this. They say that without the stimulus, more than 17 million jobs would have been lost. Which means that, instead of unemployment creeping above 10 percent, it would have peaked at around 16 percent.[38] That was the jobless rate in 1931, when soup lines stretched around the block—and just months before homeless veterans camped out on the banks of the Anacostia River near the National Mall demanding that their government provide assistance.[39]

So here's a tip for Democrats: Next time you hear someone complaining about that wasteful stimulus, with its money for new grass on the National Mall, ask them,

Question A: Because of the American Recovery and Reinvestment Act of 2009, the U.S. unemployment rate was lower at the end of 2010 than it would have been without the stimulus bill.

RESPONSES

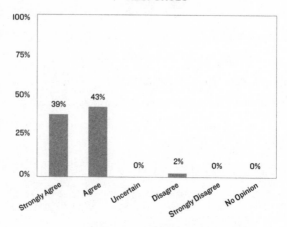

RESPONSES WEIGHTED BY EACH EXPERT'S CONFIDENCE

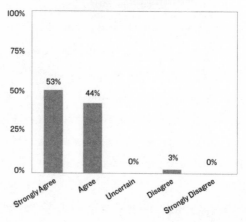

"Instead of grass, would you have preferred camps of the homeless, ready to storm federal buildings in Washington, D.C.?"

Because that, it turns out, might have been the choice alternative.

GOP INFLATION FREAK-OUT

On the morning of November 15, 2010, Ben Bernanke, the chairman of the Federal Reserve, opened *The Wall Street Journal* to find a letter addressed to him. It politely explained how he was about to ruin the country.

If you thought conservatives limited their stimulus bashing to Congress, WRONG. They took their fight to the Federal Reserve, America's central bank, which has the mission of maintaining maximum employment and a stable currency, especially in times of economic distress.

In 2010 Bernanke and the Fed were worried that the American economy was about to suffer from deflation—the opposite of inflation—when prices of goods fall. Deflation can cause a death spiral in the economy; it means companies would take in less

revenue . . . which means they'd hire fewer employees . . . which means demand for goods and services
would decrease . . . which means prices would drop
and the cycle would repeat itself.

The Fed had a plan to stop this death spiral before it got started. They called it "quantitative easing." They were going to "buy back" billions of
dollars in Treasury bonds from major banks so they
could inject cash into a sluggish economy.

Quantitative easing wasn't anything new or particularly radical. Paul Krugman, the Nobel Prize–
winning economist and *New York Times* columnist,
said it was "more of the same."[40] But Republicans
reacted as if Bernanke were about to cross the fiscal Rubicon.

A murderer's row of forty-three conservative
economists and pseudointellectuals—everyone
from Stanford's John Taylor to William Kristol—
penned an open letter, the one in the *Journal*,
saying the plan should be "reconsidered and dis-
continued." They said that, instead of preventing
deflation, quantitative easing would actually cause
the opposite crisis—it would cause prices to rise
too rapidly. In the face of economic crisis, they

were essentially calling on the Fed to pull a Herbert Hoover and do nothing.[41]

The message was echoed by the GOP political class, who built it into their party's platform. On the 2012 campaign trail in Iowa, Texas governor Rick Perry called quantitative easing "treasonous"—as if expanding the money supply was equivalent to calling for the assassination of a major American leader. In the same breath, Perry threatened the Fed chair, saying he and his fellow Texans "would treat [Bernanke] pretty ugly" if Bernanke ever came to the Lone Star State. (The irony went over Perry's head. But then again, what doesn't?)[42]

All of this ignores the fact that the naysayers' predictions never came to pass; the Fed neither spiked inflation nor wrecked the economy. In fact, it did exactly what Bernanke predicted—stopped deflation.

"By this measure," CBS's *MoneyWatch* reported, "there's no doubt that the program was a success."[43]

I don't think any of those forty-three conservatives ever wrote Bernanke to apologize. If they did, they forgot to send the letter to *The Wall Street Journal*.

SO WHAT DOES THE MANKIW TEST SAY ABOUT THE STIMULUS
versus the Republican alternative?

Well, that assumes Republicans had an alternative, that
the GOP wasn't playing politics at the very moment when
Americans were packing up their children in the middle of
the night—and driving away from their underwater mortgages. This is a difficult assumption to make.

Michael Grunwald, the ace reporter from *The Washing-*
ton Post, is an authority on the stimulus and wrote the
backslapping, backstabbing tale about how Keynes's economic theory became law—and the law became a punching bag. His book is called *The New New Deal*, and he
makes a pretty compelling case that Republicans did, indeed, use the fight over the stimulus as a way to gain back
their standing after a disastrous Bush presidency. In the
middle of an economic crisis, the GOP was bent on paint-
ing the Democrats as wasteful spenders, like teenagers
who'd stolen daddy's credit card and hitched a ride to the
mall. Grunwald reports that even when Democrats "added
language specifically banning the use of stimulus funds for
casinos, aquariums, zoos, golf courses, or swimming pools,
Republicans just asked: What about mob museums? What
about water slides? What about the Sunset View Dog Park
in Chula Vista, California?"

"We were in full kill-the-bill, let's-make-everything-famous mode," recalled one Eric Cantor aide.[44]

Hell, even if the Republicans did want to fix the economy, their alternative to the stimulus made about as much sense as tits on a bull.

Republicans actually proposed two alternatives. The first was a package about half the size of the Democrats' that contained mostly tax cuts (surprise!) and unemployment insurance. This, according to economists polled by *The New York Times*'s Eduardo Porter, would generate less commerce "than direct government spending, because households swamped by debt were likely to save their windfall."[45]

The Republicans also crafted another $715 billion alternative that would've included more infrastructure spending than the Obama stimulus. As Grunwald says, "Republicans never bothered to explain how $715 billion could be good public policy while $815 billion was freedom-crushing socialism."

As Republicans were then a minority in Congress, he adds, "They didn't have to."[46]

DEMOCRATIC Rx:

THE STIMULUS (BILLIONS IN PUBLIC SPENDING)

TAKE: SPARINGLY, AND ONLY IN CASE OF EMERGENCY.

SIDE EFFECTS: PERVASIVE SELF-DOUBT THAT YOUR MEDICATION ISN'T WORKING; AN EAR-SPLITTING HEADACHE FROM CONSERVATIVE CRITICISM; **BUT ALSO** A LATENT SENSE OF EUPHORIA THAT YOU PREVENTED THE SECOND GREAT DEPRESSION.

KEY INGREDIENTS: NINETY YEARS OF EVIDENCE THAT KEYNESIAN ECONOMICS WORK.

 REPUBLICAN Rx:

UMMMMM . . . TAX CUTS, I GUESS? OR MORE SPENDING? OR LESS SPENDING?

TAKE: UNSURE.

SIDE EFFECTS: SLOWER ECONOMIC GROWTH; GENERAL CONFUSION ABOUT WHAT WILL ACTUALLY FIX THE ECONOMY.

KEY INGREDIENTS: SNAKE OIL (WITH A GENEROUS DASH OF POLITICAL OPPORTUNISM!).

WELFARE WAR II:
PAUL RYAN'S POVERTY PLAN

The Welfare Wars have quieted down some since the Clinton days. There's no doubt that we still have a moral panic over poor unwed mothers mooching off the federal government. But I'm not sure the outrage is as outrageous as it was in 1995, when the then congressman John Mica (R-FL) brought a sign, presumably from his local zoo, onto the floor of the House of Representatives. The sign read DO NOT FEED THE ALLIGATORS.[47]

Today the Republican Party finds it less—umm, let's use the word "fashionable"—to compare poor black people to animals. This isn't to say that Trump and some of his supporters aren't vocal about their racism. They are. The folks working for Nate Silver have found that the biggest predictor of areas with Trump support are places where people google the N-word.[48] Welfare, though, hasn't been a hot-button issue.

But this could change. The Welfare Wars may soon be making a comeback, and not thanks to any fringe politician. The one itching to balance budgets on the backs of the poor is none other than the Great Conservative Hope™: Speaker of the House Paul Ryan.

If there's a wolf in sheep's clothing in the GOP, it's

Ryan. The man has a gift for wooing editorial boards, for preying on the Broderian thinking of center-left columnists who want so badly to believe that the Republican Party has a pragmatic streak. Ryan puts forward a friendly midwestern face they like and has a way of talking about issues that seems reasonable enough.

His policies, however, are anything but reasonable, and there's no harder proof of this than his plan to reduce poverty.

Since 2014, Ryan has been pitching what he calls an "opportunity grant" program with the goal of moving more welfare recipients to work. Ryan says this will make poverty programs "more accountable and more effective" while also encouraging "flexibility" and "innovation among the states."[49] Sounds great, right?

Accountability?

Flexibility?

Innovation?

ALL FANTASTIC BUZZWORDS!

Unfortunately, a policy isn't as strong as its meaningless jargon. The devil, in this case, is in the details.

The crux of Ryan's plan is that it would take eleven federal programs that currently help the poor—roughly about $100 billion in funding[50]—and put all those funds into something called a "block grant," which is money Congress gives the states for a general purpose. Under Ryan's plan,

Congress would drain the bank accounts that currently pay for everything from food stamps to housing vouchers and then basically tell the fifty states, "Here's some cash. Fight poverty however you see fit."[51]

There are plenty of reasons to be skeptical that states could more effectively combat poverty than the federal government. Just ask how the states are doing on other issues.

How did Michigan do when it re-sourced Flint's water supply?

How does Texas do when it writes the history and science chapters of its high school textbooks?

And how did Mississippi, Alabama, Louisiana, Florida, Texas, etc., etc., etc. do when they had full domain over civil rights policy?

But here's the best case against turning welfare over to the states: We already do it. And it isn't working.

A little history: In 1996 President Clinton worked with the Republican-led Congress to pass welfare reform. You might remember the sound bite: It "end[ed] welfare as we know it." The bill created something called the Temporary Assistance for Needy Families (TANF) block grant, which let states decide how best to use federal funds to move people from welfare to work. (This block grant isn't as big or broad as Paul Ryan's would be, but it fundamentally works the same way.)

The idea for TANF was a pretty good one for the late '90s, when the job market was strong, even for the poor. According to the nonpartisan Center for Budget and Policy Priorities, "TANF's early years witnessed unprecedented declines in the number of families receiving cash assistance, and unprecedented increases in the share of single mothers working, especially those with less than a high school education." But since the recession, TANF's track record has been less than stellar. For example, for every one hundred families in poverty in 1996, sixty-eight families received TANF. But by 2013, that number had dropped to twenty-six.[52]

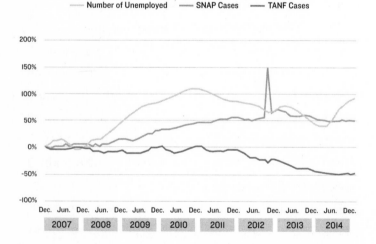

CHANGES IN TANF CASES, SNAP CASES, AND THE NUMBER OF UNEMPLOYED PERSONS IN LOUISIANA

A big reason for this is that block grants like TANF don't automatically increase as need increases—like, say, when a massive economic crisis lays off 8.7 million Americans. In fact, the number of American families in deep poverty rose by 300,000 between 1996 and 2013, but the number of families receiving TANF assistance actually *decreased* . . . by over 60 percent![53] In my home state of Louisiana, it's dropped by over 90 percent even as the poverty rate has stayed flat.[54]

Simply put, when Paul Ryan says that block grants can cure poverty, it's like saying we can cure cancer by cutting back on blood tests and chemotherapy. *The epidemic must be getting better if we're not treating it as much, right?*

But here's the worst part about handing welfare money to states—suddenly, it's not welfare money anymore!

How many times have you heard some crackpot Republican complain about welfare queens using food stamps to buy lobster or lottery tickets? If there were a hypocrisy scale, that complaint would rank near the top, somewhere around constitutional conservatives claiming there's some unwritten rule that prevents President Obama from nominating a Supreme Court justice in an election year. The hypocrisy is off the charts.

Studies show that states spend more than half of TANF dollars on things that have nothing to do with the program's core priorities. Some states use the money to plug holes in their budgets.[55] In Alaska, TANF funds ended up paying the salaries of local officials—and for the budget of a flight school in the Yukon-Kuskokwim Delta.[56] (Among the things poor Americans need most, the ability to pilot a Cessna 172 from Juneau to Anchorage is not near the top of the list.)

Then there's Mississippi, where only 15 percent of eligible poor families receive child care, and yet the state has refused to spend more TANF money on programs to help kids. Instead, they've left that money unspent.[57]

Georgia may take the cake, though. There are reports that, in an effort to cut welfare expenses, social workers often lie to needy parents, saying the state could take away their children if they apply for TANF benefits.[58]

Paul Ryan may believe he's really trying to help America's poor, and he might think that he can make states spend welfare money more wisely. "No funny business," he says.[59] If only it were that easy. The reality is that states aren't always laboratories of innovation . . . or amusement parks of accountability . . . or whatever silly-ass metaphor small-government obsessives want to use. States can be leeches, too.

The impoverished aren't mooching off their government. At the state level, their government is mooching off them.

RYAN TO POOR KIDS: LET THEM EAT CAKE!

When Paul Ryan announced his welfare proposal in 2014, he rolled it out like any "serious" policy maker would—with a boring white paper.

The first few pages detail all the *amazing* things his plan would do, like expand the Earned Income Tax Credit, but you have to slog through until page 28 to see how Ryan would pay for it. In retrospect, this was probably intentional because Ryan's pay-for is ridiculous.

He says he would partially pay for his programs that help poor people . . . by eliminating other programs that help poor people.

(Take a moment to absorb that logic.)

One of the programs Ryan would cut is the Fresh Fruit and Vegetable Program. Every year, the U.S. Department of Agriculture sets aside some money to buy poor kids fruits and vegetables, which the kids likely wouldn't have access to otherwise. A study from the University of Arkansas found that the program has "meaningfully reduced childhood obesity" among the kids it served.[60]

The program costs just $44 million a year, or about 0.0004 percent of federal welfare spending, but Ryan says it has to go because it's wasteful. More than that, he says it's a better plan than the Democrats' alternative: to marginally increase taxes on the wealthiest Americans.

Higher taxes, of course, would be too burdensome. It's better just to feed poor kids triglycerides, 7-Eleven beef jerky, and Hostess snack cakes—and pray they won't jack up Medicaid costs with all the insulin they'll need down the road.

I have to give Ryan credit for making history, though. He may be the first government leader since Marie Antoinette to say of poor people, "Let them eat cake!"

THE DIVIDE ON WELFARE IS VERY CLEAR: FOR MORE THAN A generation, Republicans have seen welfare as a form of charity and tried to wean the poor off of it as fast as possible, often to the detriment of the neediest Americans.

I think of welfare differently. I see welfare not as charity, but as an investment—an investment in some of the country's most shit-out-of-luck individuals, but individuals with as much God-given potential as you or me. And there's no better example of this than the food stamp program.

DEMOCRATIC Rx:

WELFARE AS AN INVESTMENT

TAKE: FROM BIRTH UNTIL NO LONGER NEEDED.

SIDE EFFECTS: HIGHER-ACHIEVING POOR PEOPLE; A HEALTH-IER, HAPPIER POPULATION.

KEY INGREDIENTS: THE UNDERSTANDING THAT PEOPLE ARE ON WELFARE NOT BY CHOICE BUT BY NECESSITY, AND NEED SOCI-ETY TO INVEST IN THEM BEFORE THEY CAN INVEST IN SOCIETY.

A recent study from economists at UC Berkeley, Columbia University, and Northwestern University found that the earlier poor children have access to food stamps, the better off they are as adults. Children whose families used food stamps graduated high school at higher rates, earned more as adults, and were less likely to develop health issues like diabetes, obesity, and heart disease.

"Because these individuals are healthier and more financially sound, the benefits also pay out to taxpayers. Healthier Americans lead to less cost when it comes to future health care for the average taxpayer," the study concluded. "Our findings suggest that the [food stamp] bene-

REPUBLICAN Rx:

GIVE ALL THE WELFARE MONEY TO THE STATES!

TAKE: ALL MONEY FROM THE FEDERAL COFFERS AND SEND IT TO THE STATES.

SIDE EFFECTS: INCREASED POVERTY; MISAPPROPRIATION OF FUNDS; A LIKELY OUTBREAK OF HYPOCRISY AMONG "FISCALLY CONSERVATIVE" STATE LEGISLATORS.

KEY INGREDIENTS: SNAKE OIL (NOT AVAILABLE FOR PURCHASE WITH FOOD STAMPS).

fits that go to children are better thought of as an investment rather than as charity."[61]

I couldn't agree more.

THE RATTLESNAKE KINGS

Let me wrap up this chapter with a bit of unusual history.

In 1893, at the World's Fair, in Chicago, a former cowboy named Clark Stanley faced the crowd before him, reached into his knapsack, and pulled out a rattlesnake, which he then promptly slit with his knife from head to tail. The crowd watched the juices leak out.

Stanley was marketing his new cure-all, a liniment supposedly made from serpent juices. It was supposed to alleviate all the aches and pains after a hard day's work. He called it "Stanley's Snake Oil," and it grew so popular that Stanley was bestowed the nickname the "Rattlesnake King."

Thousands of suckers lined up to buy Stanley's product, but unfortunately for them, it didn't contain any curative properties. Hell, it didn't even include a drop of actual snake oil, whatever that is. When the authorities studied Stanley's medicine, they found that it was made from a combination of beef fat, red pepper, and turpentine. And Stanley's legacy became not that of a healer but of a huckster.

He inadvertently coined the phrase "snake oil."[62]

When Republicans talk about the founders of their party, they mention several names: Abraham Lincoln, Dwight Eisenhower, Barry Goldwater, and Ronald Reagan. But to my mind, no historical figure is more responsible for the Republican Party's current policies and politics than Clark Stanley, the Rattlesnake King.

The Republicans sell their economic policies in the same way Stanley sold his snake oil. Whether it's tax cuts for the rich or slashing spending, they market their policies as cures for everyone. They say their ideas are good for all Americans, even though the benefits—if there are benefits—go to very, very few people. "Just take a couple of drops of a tax cut for the 1 percent," they say. "And even if you're not part of the 1 percent, you'll feel better."

I want to be very clear: This is some old-fashioned hucksterism. We now have twenty years of evidence on job creation, tax cuts, spending cuts, and welfare reform, and all of the proof shows Republican ideas to be no better than colored turpentine in a bottle.

I would respect the GOP a hell of a lot more if they were just honest, if they didn't pretend tax cuts for the wealthy helped the middle class. I wouldn't mind so much if they just said, "We think rich people should get to keep the money."

I wouldn't agree with that idea, but at least it's a real argument they can make.

 THE McCAIN AWARD FOR STUPIDITY INVOLVING THE AMERICAN ECONOMY

Y'all remember what John McCain said about the economy during the 2008 presidential campaign, right? In the midst of the greatest financial crisis since the Great Depression, the Republican nominee for president told the nation, "The fundamentals of the economy are strong." The nation then watched that economy shed 9 million jobs and the GDP go into a tailspin.

In retrospect, McCain's comment was, without a doubt, the most ill-advised statement about the U.S. economy made during the post–George W. Bush era. And in McCain's honor, I've decided to name an award after him. It's for the politician who offers the most idiotic comment or prediction about the prosperity and commerce of the United States.

Here are my rankings for the first official McCain Award for Stupidity Involving the American Economy:

FIFTH RUNNER-UP: NEWT GINGRICH

former Speaker of the House and 2012 presidential candidate

"It's very clear that under Obama's job-killing policies, we're not going to get out of this deep unemployment." (July 10, 2011)[63]

Newt has a track record of making bad predictions about the economy. In 1993, he believed the country would fall into recession within a year's time and that it would be "the Democrat machine's recession, and each one of them will be held personally accountable."[64] The country then proceeded to undergo the most fantastic economic growth in a half century.

Anyway, Newt's comment about the Obama economy was no more prescient. Since July 2011, when he said "we're never going to get out of this deep unemployment," the American economy has added millions of jobs and the unemployment rate has dropped from 9.1 percent to 5 percent.[65]

FOURTH RUNNER–UP: BILL KRISTOL

editor of *The Weekly Standard*

"[Kansas governor Sam Brownback's] success may be such that he will get more and more attention. A re-elected Sam Brownback in early 2015 is a formidable presidential possibility." (December 29, 2012)[66]

Bill Kristol is the editor of the conservative magazine *The Weekly Standard* and is most recently known for trying to recruit someone—anyone—to run as a third-party conservative candidate against Donald Trump. Kristol has mentioned a lot of potential candidates, including Mitt Romney. But I found it interesting that one name he never uttered was Sam Brownback's, the man who was supposed to be such a "formidable" contender.

This is probably because Sam Brownback has

run his state into the ground since Kristol made his prediction. Unbridled conservatism has left Kansas in a state of near bankruptcy. In fact, I'd wager that today, "Brownback for America" would be less popular than a presidential ticket of Genital Herpes and the reanimated corpse of Joseph Goebbels.

Kristol was right about one thing, though: Brownback has gotten "more and more attention," but it hasn't been due to his success.

THIRD RUNNER-UP: MITT ROMNEY

"I believe the Bush tax cuts helped our economy grow and are one of the reasons that we're not in a recession today." (January 6, 2008;[67] one month after the National Bureau of Economic Research says the recession began)

Romney's best-known bad prediction about the economy is that the auto bailout would fail. But for my money, the above quote takes the cake. In the fifteen years since Bush lowered taxes (mostly for the very rich), economists have roundly criticized the policy for costing way too much and generating too little growth. Saying the Bush tax cuts kept us out of a recession in 2008—right at the beginning of the crisis—is like feeling your left arm go numb and then saying, "I believe my diet of McDonald's and scotch is one of the reasons I haven't had a heart attack."

SECOND RUNNER-UP: DONALD TRUMP

"Well, I think Wall Street's waiting to see what happens [with the Iraq war]. . . . It looks like a tremendous success from a military standpoint and I think this is really nothing compared to what you're gonna see after the war is over. . . . I think Wall Street's just gonna go up like a rocket, even beyond, and it's gonna continue and, you know, we have a strong and powerful country and let's hope it all works out." (March 21, 2003, one day into the invasion of Iraq)[68]

Trump claims that he was (1) against the war in Iraq and that (2) he's a businessman of tremendous foresight and savvy. Well, this statement basically takes a kitchen knife straight to the heart of both of those arguments. Trump not only supported the war in Iraq—he told Howard Stern in 2002 that he was for it—Trump also thought the Iraq War would be good for the economy!

WINNER: BOBBY JINDAL

former Louisiana governor

"We have balanced our budget eight years in a row without raising taxes. Largest tax cut in our state's history. Income tax cut. Secondly, we have cut our state budget 26 percent, $9 billion. Cut over 30,000 state government bureaucrats. We've actually had eight credit upgrades. Our highest credit rating in decades. We've got more people working than ever before in Louisiana's history, earning a higher income than ever before. We reversed 25 years of out-migration, seven years in a row of in-migration. Actually, you look at Louisiana's economy, we have got $60 billion, 90,000 jobs coming into our state because of economic development wins." (July 12, 2015)[69]

That's right, Governor Bobby Jindal wins the McCain Award for Stupidity Involving the American Economy.

To be honest, Jindal had home-field advantage in this competition. After all, he is the governor of Louisiana, my home state. But make no mistake, Jindal is absolutely deserving of this award because the above comment couldn't be more misleading if it included a treasure map to Hell. Jindal's record in Louisiana has been abysmal.

From the moment he entered the Louisiana governor's mansion in 2009, Jindal enacted policies as ridiculously conservative as those in Kansas—massive slashes to public spending and tax cuts for the rich—and the results have been equally disastrous. Jindal turned a near 1-billion-dollar surplus into a 1.6-billion-dollar deficit by the time he left office. He blew an $800-million-dollar hole in the state's budget with tax cuts for the rich in the country's second-poorest state, and to make up that gap, Jindal slashed social services.[70]

Today, Louisiana can no longer afford to provide public defenders for all its criminal defendants. It's being reported that the Department of Children and Family Services will soon no longer have the money to investigate child abuse. And the state's hospitals are likely to see at least $64 million in funding cuts this year.[71]

I often say that Hurricane Katrina was the worst thing to happen to Louisiana. But Bobby Jindal has made a strong case for himself.

America Isn't What It Used to Be

This is a chapter about one of the biggest problems facing America, and I want to kick it off in the typical Carville way, with a good ol'-fashioned, foam-at-the-mouth (or, in this case, foam-at-the-keyboard) rant.

It's a rant about a phrase that you couldn't escape if you followed the Republican primary contest.

The phrase is: *America isn't what it used to be.*

SAY WHAT YOU WILL ABOUT TRUMP SUPPORTERS—AND I'VE said it all—but these folks aren't supporting a talking honey-baked ham with authoritarian inclinations for no reason. These people have grievances. They don't like the way the country has changed over the past eight years—probably longer than that. So they go to the rallies. And they buy the stupid red hats that read MAKE AMERICA GREAT AGAIN. Because to them, America is not what it used to be.

And, boy, don't I know it.

See, I fall right in The Donald's demographic sweet spot. I'm a bald white Southern veteran who's known for yelling about politics. I look just like your drunk uncle, except chances are that I'm even drunker. But most important, I was born during a time that Donald fondly calls "the good old days."

My momma brought me into this world in 1944, and by the time I was in elementary school, Germany was a ruin and Japan was on its ass. Meanwhile, I was living in a town that was named for my granddaddy (Carville, Louisiana), in a state that preferred my race (white), and in a country where the odds were that I'd die richer than my parents (Chester and Miss Nippy).

So every morning I skipped to school like Little Lord Fauntleroy. The world was mine to run. Even three decades later in 1973, when I graduated from LSU law school, my class portrait looked like a Trump rally—a sea of white guys dotted with three women and one African American. We were the photo negative of diversity.

And yet, whenever I hear that phrase—*America isn't what it used to be*—I don't nod and reminisce. You won't catch me waxing nostalgic about the good ol' days. Instead, my response is: "No shit! Of course America isn't what it used to be."

And why is that a problem?

The worst part of the Trump phenomenon—well, all the parts are the worst part—but a particularly bad aspect of The Donald's movement is that it gets this question wrong. He doesn't understand that America isn't what it used to be, and in so many ways THIS IS A GOOD THING.

After all, America used to be Jim Crow and White Flight and Black Lung.

America used to be stationed at the Berlin Wall and in the Ia Drang Valley.

America used to be a place where seniors died poor, and the poor died in the streets.

Team Trump looks at all this change and dismisses it. They don't seem to care that the 1950s weren't exactly a prime time to be alive if you were black, gay, Hispanic, an immigrant, disabled, non-Christian, or a woman—anybody but a white man, really. In fact, if you look at the issues where Trump has distinguished himself—a wall on the Mexican border, a trade war with China, the banning of Muslims, and the rumored Kenyan birth of our president—it's hard to say he doesn't want to take us back to a blustery and bigoted America. He envisions a presidency that's half Clint

Eastwood from *Dirty Harry*, half Clint Eastwood from *Gran Torino*.

For me, this answers the question of whether Trump and his supporters are "real conservatives." You bet your sweet ass they are. William Buckley, the intellectual forefather of conservatism, once said a conservative is someone who "stands athwart history, yelling, 'STOP!'" And if that's the measure we're using, Trump supporters are slightly to the right of Genghis Khan. They're not just telling history to stop; they're telling it to "back the hell up!"—except for the one part of our history we should return to.

This is an important point: Because there really is one way that America isn't like it used to be, and it's a damn shame. There is one change we should reverse, but it has nothing to do with Trump's views. It has nothing to do with immigrants. Or Muslims. Or China. Or Obama. It's something else entirely, and I'll give you one guess what it is.

How many times do I have to say it? *It's the economy, stupid!*

Specifically, there are two trends at work in the American economy that, if unaddressed, threaten to take the whole enterprise under. The two trends are:

- The middle class has effectively gone without a pay raise since the mid-1970s. Real wages have increased little if at all for most Americans.[1]

- At the same time, wealth in this country is becoming increasingly concentrated in the hands of fewer and fewer people. Wages for the top 1 percent have risen 165 percent, and wages for the top 0.1 percent have risen 362 percent.[2]

When economists and politicians talk about "rising income inequality," these are the trends they're talking about.

WE LIKE TO THINK OF AMERICAN HISTORY AS A STRAIGHT LINE, a wagon train that heads in only one direction—forward. We believe it was a smooth path from colony to superpower, from trading posts on the frontier to the tech campuses of Silicon Valley. The march of progress, we think, has continued uninterrupted, without pit stops or wrong turns.

But all that's a damn lie.

The fact is: When it comes to income inequality, the United States is getting worse, not better. The march of progress is going in reverse. The wagon train is infected with diphtheria. Or whatever.

Income inequality is the one thing that makes it hard not to get nostalgic about the good old days. In the 2008 campaign, John McCain was rightly ripped to shreds for saying "The fundamentals of the economy are strong," but for most of McCain's lifetime (and mine), that statement was spot-on. Ours was a country where the fundamentals of the economy were strong—and strong for everyone. In the three decades following World War II, the wealthiest 20 percent of American families saw their incomes double. So did the poorest 20 percent and everyone in between.[3]

It was an unbelievable cycle of prosperity. The more people who rose into the middle class, the more demand there was for the cars and appliances that other middle-class workers were producing. The economy just kept growing, creating millions of jobs.

But about the time we pulled out of Vietnam—not long after they snapped my class portrait at LSU Law—something started to change. Prosperity no longer was widely shared. Instead, the rich got far richer, the poor got poorer, and the middle class experienced a real-life version of the trash compactor scene from the original *Star Wars*.

By the mid-1990s, income inequality was an obvious and incoming threat. If the U.S. Bureau of Labor and Statistics had been outfitted with alarms like the Pentagon, the red sirens would've been blaring. The statistics in 1993 showed that the top 20 percent of earners had seen their incomes rise by almost a fifth over the prior two decades. But during that same amount of time, the bottom 20 percent of earners had effectively experienced a 20 percent *pay cut*.[4]

For a while, America was able to grit its teeth through the pain. Mothers went to work in increasing numbers, turning one-income families into two-income families; homeowners took out mortgages using their houses as credit cards to soften the blow of income inequality. But when the bubble burst in 2008 and the recession hit, there was no cushion left. People started feeling the data.

Today income inequality in America is greater than at any point since 1928—before the Great Depression. The bottom 90 percent of Americans now control less than half of the country's wealth, and even worse, they're capturing far less of the new wealth that's being created. Hedge-fund managers may accuse Obama of perpetuating "class war-

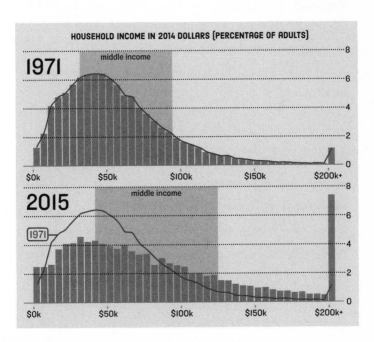

fare," but the real perpetrator of the rich-versus-poor divide isn't the president or his rhetoric; it's an economic recovery that has benefited very wealthy Americans and screwed over the working class.

The easiest way to see income inequality at work is like this: Imagine that we could shrink America down to one hundred people. (Something that might actually happen if Donald Trump gets his child-sized hands on the nuclear trigger, but that's another story for another day.) In this tiny America, with a population of one hundred, the richest individual would've received almost all the wealth created during the economic recovery from 2009 to 2013. Of every ten dollars generated, he would've pocketed about $9.10.[5]

That leaves just ninety cents—three quarters, a dime, and a nickel—for the remaining ninety-nine Americans to scrap over.

OF COURSE, LIFE ISN'T SUPPOSED TO BE FAIR. NOR IS A FREE-market economy. But this level of inequality isn't a problem because it's "unfair." No serious politician—not even a Democrat—expects every worker to earn the same as the richest American. But we do expect everyone to have a fair chance at improving their lot in life. And that's the problem with income inequality; it takes that chance and crushes it.

Income inequality isn't an issue of fairness. It's an issue of opportunity.

Today we're a country where 1 percent of the population captures 90 percent of the new wealth. And if that statistic seems like it belongs to a banana republic or an Eastern European dictatorship—and not the United States of America—it's no coincidence. In the most recent analysis from the Organization for Economic Cooperation and Development (OECD), America's inequality level ranks closest to Turkey's, a country where about 13 percent of the people don't have access to an indoor flushing toilet and yet their leader is rumored to crap upon a golden commode.[6] (Is there a better metaphor for inequality than a gold toilet? I don't think so.)

Now, my point is *not* that America is the next Turkey or Jamaica or Argentina, all of which are countries with roughly the same level of income inequality. America is the world's lone superpower. There is no way 13 percent of us are going to lose our indoor plumbing anytime soon.

That said, inequality is grinding away at what makes us exceptional compared to other nations. Look at Turkey as an example. In Turkey, if your father was a pomegranate farmer—and a lot of people's fathers there are—chances are that you will end up a pomegranate farmer, too, living a similar life. On the other hand, if your father was a petroleum oligarch, you will be prepared for a life of equestrian lessons and ivory towers. There'd always be an umbrella in your drink and a lot of digits in your bank account. You'd probably never even cross paths with the kid of the pomegranate farmer.

The reason isn't complicated. When a country has significant income inequality, a large chunk of the population can't afford the things necessary for economic advancement—things like a safe neighborhood, modern health care, reliable transportation, and a solid (and low-debt) education.

All of those things are the rungs needed to climb an economic ladder. When they are harder to afford, the rungs are farther apart, and the ladder is more difficult to climb. Sure, the farmer's kid could theoretically jump to the top rung of that ladder. Maybe he wins the lottery. Maybe he happens to be a genius who can teach himself advanced biochemistry by candlelight, and he puts the petroleum oligarch out of business. But let's be realistic. Without education or health care or any of those other advantages, it's far more likely that he'll just die in a house similar to the one in which he was born. He'll stay a pomegranate farmer.

This is why so many people around the world have flocked to America. Because America has always been the place where the rungs on the ladder are close together.

We've been a country where you didn't have to win the MegaMillions or have a one-in-a-billion IQ to eke out a better life for yourself. America is a nation where grit can help you climb just as high as luck or genius.

At least that used to be the case.

Economists differ on the long-term effects of high levels of income inequality in the United States, but almost all agree that the rungs on our ladder are getting farther apart. Americans are increasingly finding it harder to climb. A child born in the top 20 percent today has about a two-in-three chance of staying at or near the top, but a kid born into the bottom 20 percent has a less than one-in-twenty shot at making it to the top. He is ten times likelier to stay where he is at the bottom of the ladder.[7]

I didn't support Bernie Sanders during the Democratic primaries, but I give him a lot of credit for bringing attention to this issue. Economists have been ringing alarm bells about income inequality's broader effects on society for years. There's one French economist in particular—his name is Thomas Piketty—whose ideas on income inequality have swept through the economics community since he published a book in 2013. Piketty's book is titled *Capital in the Twenty-First Century*, and it's become an instant classic—albeit one with some very scary implications. Piketty has spent his entire career studying the Gilded Age, an era in the nineteenth century when classes were rigid and upward mobility was impossible to achieve. Think about the novels of Charles Dickens—all the characters were obsessed with marrying rich or receiving a surprise inheritance because there was no other way to improve your lot in life. All new wealth flowed to the already wealthy. Barring a miracle, the poor stayed poor.

Piketty believes the world economy could be returning to a time like this, a Second Gilded Age, an era when everyone is on a ladder that can't be climbed.[8]

SO THE QUESTION IS: WHO'S GOING TO STEP UP AND REBUILD the ladder?

Well, you might reasonably think it's the Republicans.

John Steinbeck, the author of *The Grapes of Wrath*, famously said that "socialism never took root in America because the poor see themselves . . . as temporarily embarrassed millionaires." And since Reagan, Republicans have exploited this idea—that all Americans, no matter their wealth, are merely temporarily embarrassed millionaires. This is why everyone should admire the rich and support low taxes for the wealthy because soon they, too, will be back on top. That's the conservative argument at least.

So you might expect that the GOP would take income inequality seriously, that they'd see it as a big threat to their blue-collar voters, who now look less like temporarily embarrassed millionaires and more like permanently depressed low earners. But no.

Instead, the Republican Party has gone through a tortured process while coming to accept that income inequality is real and a problem. I'm no therapist, but it reminds me of the five stages of grief.

You might be familiar with the five stages of grief. A psychiatrist named Elisabeth Kübler-Ross came up with the theory that there are five emotions you experience before accepting death. And Republicans seem to be experiencing all of them over the death of the middle class. In fact, if Dr. Kübler-Ross were able to examine the GOP, I bet she'd find that Republicans were feeling all five emotions at once. (Thank God Obamacare covers therapy, huh?)

THE GOP'S FIVE STAGES OF GRIEF: INCOME-INEQUALITY EDITION

1. DENIAL

The first stage of grief, according to Dr. Kübler-Ross, is denying that something is wrong. Twenty years ago, when I started researching *We're Right, They're Wrong*, that's exactly what conservatives did. They denied income inequality was a problem. One *Washington Post* columnist actually said that our country was becoming *more* equal. His proof, and I'm not kidding about this, was that most homes were "increasingly stocked with middle class gadgets . . . 58 percent have telephone answering machines."[9]

There you have it, folks. Income inequality can't exist because of . . . well, you get the message . . . voice mail.

You'd think people would've wised up by now, but conservatives are a little slow on the uptake. Compared with Democrats and independents, majorities of which say the economy is becoming increasingly unfair, 55 percent of Republicans think otherwise. They believe the economy is "fair." Four in ten Republicans believe the wealth gap is either a small problem—or not a problem whatsoever.[10]

In other words, in any conservative crowd—from a Hamptons clambake to the Republican National Convention—you're probably going to find more people who think Caitlyn Jenner is a bigger problem than the impending doom of the middle class.

2. ANGER

The next step in the grieving process is anger, which is not really a feeling for Republicans so much as a perpetual state of existence. Conservatives go purple with rage over everything from the president's golf game, to Cam Newton's touchdown dance, to the gay couple on *Modern Family*, to, of course, anyone who has the gall to say something non-Christian like "Happy holidays." Bring up income inequality, however, and they'll kick their anger up a notch. They'll act like you're going to drain their bank account and give the money to the reanimated corpse of Vladimir Lenin. *It's class warfare!*

The best (or, uh, worst) example of this was a 2011 segment from Bill O'Reilly's show. The clip was subtly titled "Will Violent Class Warfare Break Out in the USA?" Bill was commenting on riots in Great Britain and predicted that street violence would soon come to America because of all the talk about income inequality. "Some people believe that tax cuts for the rich are harming the economy," Bill said, pointing to a poll in which most Americans called for higher taxes for the wealthy. "That poll will certainly fuel class warfare," he concluded, while pictures of rioting mobs and burning cars rolled on-screen.[11]

Five years later, Bill still fumes about income inequality, which he calls "a giant ruse designed to get votes for the Democratic Party."[12] I am not a regular guest on Bill's program anymore, and I seem to have lost his e-mail address, so I've decided to write him an open letter with my response.

> *Dear Bill,*
>
> *For the last several years, I've watched you discuss income inequality while trying to vent the steam rising out of your forehead.*
>
> *I understand that you are angry about discussions of the wealth gap in America, which you*

think is "a giant ruse" designed to get votes. But trust me, Bill, if Democrats wanted more votes, we wouldn't have to invent the concept of income inequality to get them.

In fact, having spent many Saturday nights at casinos near the Mississippi River, I know there's only one thing liberals have to do to secure the ballots of disaffected low-income baby boomers. We just have to pass a law that lets them deposit their Social Security checks right into a slot machine. We'd paint the South blue for a generation.

Anyway, Bill, you should also know that polls don't lead to class warfare. I know you said they do, but they don't. In fact, polls don't lead the public to do anything. Because polls already reflect the way the public is feeling. This is how polls work. And the polls say that on the issue of income inequality, Americans are feeling frustrated.

I understand this worries you. You're afraid that discussing the wealth gap will cause riots. I can assure you, Bill, this will not happen.

Talking about income inequality will not lead to a riot, but refusing to do something about it probably will.

Sincerely,
James

3. BARGAINING

Kübler-Ross says that when death comes a-knockin', those dying call on the good Lord to strike a deal. For example, *If you let me live, God, I'll never drink again* or *If you spare me, I'll donate all my income to the Blessed Sisters of Perpetual Chastity and build homes in Guatemala with my callused bare hands.*

In psychiatry, they call this "bargaining."

In politics, it's called a "George Will column."

Somewhere along the line, conservatives began to bargain with the idea of income inequality. They didn't ask that America be spared from the widening rich-versus-poor divide, only that the wealth gap wouldn't work out so bad for the country. They pled for a miracle: *If income inequality must exist, Lord, then let it be a good thing!*

No one has captured that argument better than George Will, the archconservative columnist. When I was researching my first book in 1996, he said that the wealth gap might actually be a positive development for America. George wrote that a "society that values individualism, enterprise, and a market economy is neither surprised or scandalized when the unequal distribution of marketable skills produces large disparities in the distribution of wealth."[13]

Twenty years later, George Will is even more convinced. He believes that America's problem with income inequality is that we don't have enough! "Income inequality in a capitalist system is truly beautiful," George wrote in *The Wash-ington Post.*

Yes, you read that correctly—"income inequality is *beautiful.*" Mr. Will describes the wealth divide with a word most people reserve for their wife. He's in loooove with it.

George's rationale—I am not making this up—is that everyone is better off when money is in fewer hands be-cause billionaires and monopolies are very good at finding cheap labor in China. This means that products cost less. "Americans . . . get a raise when they shop at the store that made Sam Walton a billionaire," he says. "Since 2000, the price of a 50-inch plasma TV has fallen from $20,000 to $550."[14]

So there you have it. Conservatives would trade away the middle class and the American dream . . . all so every-one can watch *CSI: Miami* in high def.

Now that's what I call a bargain.

4. ~~DEPRESSION~~ DELUSION

Yes, I know the fourth stage of the Kübler-Ross model is "depression," and not "delusion." But the Republicans have a unique inability to feel sorry for themselves even when they should. So "delusion" is what we have to work with. Sorry, Dr. Kübler-Ross.

For more than six years of his presidency, George W. Bush was stuck in the denial stage over income inequality.

In fact, the *Washington Post* reviewed all of W.'s public remarks and found that until 2007, there was no record that he ever uttered the words "income" and "inequality" next to each other.[15] This is somewhat impressive when you consider all the other words Bush managed to pair up, like "Saddam" and "WMDs," or "mission" and "accomplished."

But when the Democrats torched Republicans in the 2006 midterms, partially over the issue of income inequality, Bush was forced to confront the issue. He did so at the tail end of a speech, which he began by praising the tax cuts he created.[16] This is sort of like the tobacco industry complaining about lung cancer or El Chapo denouncing America's narcotics problem. You can't be against a problem if *you* are the cause of the problem! And the Bush tax cuts certainly have been a real part of the cause of rising income inequality. The data show that those tax cuts made the gap between the rich and the poor worse, with the top 1 percent of earners receiving 30 percent of the benefits.[17]

It was absolutely delusional to support regressive tax cuts like Bush's and, at the same time, talk about the problem of income inequality. And yet, Republicans still do it. Even Trump's plan would cut taxes for the wealthy while doing comparatively little for the middle class and poor. The Tax Policy Center found that the average low-income taxpayer would get an extra $128 a year from Trump's

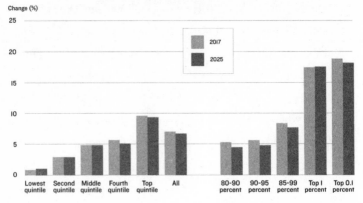

PERCENT CHANGE IN AFTER–TAX INCOME UNDER TRUMP PROPOSAL

By expanded cash income percentile, 2017 and 2025

plan, but the average top 1 percenter would get $275,257, and the average 0.1 percenter would get $1.3 million.[18]

The GOP's delusion needs immediate medical intervention.

5. ACCEPTANCE (DEATH)

Ah, the final stage—death. Adios. Game over. The fat lady sings.

We've already established that for Republicans, the Grim Reaper appeared in the form of a spray tan with a comb-over.

Death, thy name is Donald Trump.

I've written about how Donald Trump has buried the

GOP. But income inequality is a big part of the reason that someone with a nasal Queens accent became a leading presidential contender. The canyon between rich and poor is growing, and Trump's rank-and-file supporters are many of the folks who feel like they're falling into the chasm. Most of Trump's supporters during the primary didn't have a college degree that might carry them to the next level of employment. And even though most Trump voters made more than the average American, they skewed toward the poorer side of Republican voters. A third made under $50,000 a year.[19]

In retrospect, it's no wonder that these voters bolted for Trump. For twenty years, the GOP has been struggling with the issue of income inequality, and its conservative policies make it harder for working-class folks to get ahead. Trump stepped onto the political stage and offered an answer.

Unfortunately, it was the wrong answer.

ANYONE WHO FOLLOWED THE GOP PRIMARY KNOWS THAT fact-checking Donald Trump is like arguing with a five-year-old—*you're always right, but does it really matter?* Trump, it's fair to say, doesn't have a firm grasp on policy details; he doesn't even pretend to. So I won't exhaust many brain cells discussing his proposals, mostly because Trump hasn't exhausted many brain cells thinking about them either.

But I do want to address two issues that have captured the attention of working-class voters—illegal immigration and bad trade deals. Because people say these are often the big-time causes of income inequality. And that's just not true.

MEXICANS ARE "TAKING OUR MONEY"

TRUMP: "[Mexico is] killing us at the border . . . They're taking our jobs. They're taking our manufacturing jobs. They're taking our money. They're killing us."[20]

TRUTH: If Mexico is "killing us at the border," then immigrants must be pouring through. So let's start this off with a question—*How many more illegal Mexican immigrants live in America today compared to 2009 when Obama took office?*

A. 5,000
B. 10,000
C. 50,000
D. -140,000.

The correct response is D. And, no, the minus sign isn't a typo.

Between 2009 and 2014, the number of illegal Mexican immigrants in the United States actually *dropped* by 140,000. More illegal immigrants crossed the Mexican border heading in the direction of Juárez than toward Austin. Which means that the only thing a border wall would do is keep more illegal immigrants *in America*. So, no. Mexico is not "killing us at the border." Nor is any other nation for that matter. Since 2009, illegal immigration, regardless of the country of origin, has been flat.[21]

For the sake of argument, however, let's assume that America's immigration problem was getting worse; would that increase income inequality?

The vast majority of economists answer with a resounding no. But again, for the sake of argument, let's listen to the few who say yes. Is immigration a big driver of income inequality?

Well, George Borjas, an economist from Harvard who Republicans often cite, found the following: If we stopped all immigration—legal and illegal—from 1990 on, then American high school dropouts would've seen a 3.1 percent increase in their income over the long run. (High school graduates, on the other hand, would have seen their incomes actually *decline* without immigration).[22]

Here's the bottom line: If we had closed our borders, then a high school dropout earning $20,000 might've made $20,620. Six hundred bucks isn't nothing, but the working class isn't aching just because of a theoretical 3 percent decrease in income. The National Bureau of Economic Research estimates that immigration accounted for only about one-twentieth of the reason for wage inequality from 1980 to 2000.[23]

And remember, that data includes both illegal immigrants and legal immigrants, one of whom is married to Donald Trump.

"I'D LOVE TO HAVE A TRADE WAR WITH CHINA"

TRUMP: "I'd love to have a trade war with China . . . because if we did no business with China, we will save a lot of money. We're losing a fortune to China."[24]

TRUTH: If you listen to Donald Trump, you'd come away with the impression that the people negotiating America's trade deals sniffed a lot of glue and were dropped on their heads as children. "We have incompetent people negotiating trade," Trump says.

Trump's solution is simple. All he needs to do is

bring the Chinese back to the negotiating table, poke his finger straight in the middle of President Xi Jinping's chest, and demand a better deal. And if the Chinese don't bite, then we go to war—trade war. Trump has proposed slapping a 45 percent tariff on imports from China and Japan, and a 35 percent tariff on goods from Mexico.

Well, let's set aside the fact that the United States doesn't even have a trade deal with China, so there's nothing to renegotiate. The data show that free-trade deals actually *make money* for America. Among countries where we have free-trade agreements, the United States is generating a $56 billion trade surplus just in manufactured goods.[25]

Look. There's no doubt that globalization and the opening of foreign markets has made life harder for certain Americans, especially blue-collar workers. They aren't making too many pipe fittings in Garbutt, New York, anymore. That work has gone elsewhere. But you have to be sniffing glue yourself to believe that a trade war is the best way to help folks affected by globalization.

According to a study from the nonpartisan National Foundation for American Policy, "Donald Trump's proposed tariffs on China, Mexico and, by implication, Japan would be ineffective in shielding American workers from foreign imports, since producers from other countries would export the same products to the United States. Were such tariffs to be 'effective,' then the tariffs would impose a regressive consumption tax of $11,100 over 5 years on the typical U.S. household."

The study also says that "the impact would hit poor Americans the hardest: A tariff of 45% on imports from China and Japan and 35% on Mexican imports would cost U.S. households in the lowest 10% of income up to 18% of their (mean) after-tax income or $4,670 over 5 years."[26]

An 18 percent cut in the poorest families' incomes? I'm going to start calling that the Trump Stupidity Tax.

HERE ARE THE FACTS: THERE IS NO QUICK-AND-DIRTY SOLU-tion for fixing income inequality. A border wall or a trade war will not suddenly revive the working class. If you believe otherwise, I have the e-mail address of a Nigerian prince who'd like your bank account number.

Believe me, I wish this was not the case. I wish income inequality could be solved with a single silver bullet. But income inequality defies simple fixes because it isn't like a tumor that can be cut cleanly out; it cannot be excised from our economic system. Its causes are tangled up in all the ways our modern society works.

For two decades, economists have been punching away at their calculators trying to trace the cause of the wealth gap back to the root, and the roots, they've found, go everywhere. According to Thomas Piketty, who said that the working class is falling into a trap where they can't get ahead, the trap is set because of big historic forces. The global economy, of which everyone is a part, is growing slower than the profits people can make from "capital," things like factories and investments—things not many people have. And all of this, in turn, is being driven by even larger forces: the fact that the growth of the working-age population is slowing and that new technologies aren't producing the same kind of broad-based wealth they used to. To reverse these changes would be like reversing the tides or rewinding history. It's beyond the power of any one country, let alone any one president. What America can do, however, is adapt itself to meet this new world.[27]

I often take Democrats to the woodshed for not being clear enough in their messaging. (The slogan "It's the economy, stupid" isn't exactly a tagline that you need a public-policy PhD to parse.) But then again, complexity isn't always a bad thing in politics. A lot of the time it's a necessary thing, and income inequality is one of those times. It's also a case where Democrats—especially our 2016 nominee for president—get it right.

One of the things that I respect most about Hillary Clinton is that she doesn't try to dumb down the issue of income inequality, even though it's been very effective for others like Trump to do so. She understands income inequality doesn't lend itself to easy short-term solutions. Fixing the persistent opportunity gap is the work of a generation, and it requires doing everything from making education more affordable to making the wealthy pay a fairer share of taxes.

At the same time, Hillary also understands we're not going to transform a fifty-year-old former steelworker into a computer programmer overnight. Which is why she supports raising the minimum wage and giving tax breaks to companies that share profits with their employees. [28]

I know these aren't the sexiest solutions. They're not as tangible as a border wall or as rage quenching as cursing a Mexican trade delegation. But sexy isn't the point. Being effective is. And that's something Democrats haven't lost sight of.

I'm not sure how I'd convince an audience of Trump supporters that we're right about this. As I said, this book isn't really about convincing them, but I'll give it my best shot nonetheless. Here's what I would say:

I understand that many of you support Donald Trump because you feel that America isn't what you expected it would be. Your life has been harder than you planned. I get that.

I don't support Donald Trump. I find his ideas about race and religion and immigration and many other things to be toxic and the worst of what America has to offer. So if you like those aspects of his campaign, there's the door. Democracy is about getting the most votes, but we don't want yours. The politician in me doesn't approve of that. But the moralist in me sure does.

For those of you still here, you might want to hear about how to make America "what it used to be." But I can't do that either. Because America was never what it used to be.

Yes, you may have been born into a country where you felt a stable job and a living wage was your birthright. But America changes. It always has.

Before us, there was a generation who was told they wouldn't be required to fight foreign wars—and then came 1914 and 1941.

Before them, there was a generation that was told they could earn their living off the backs of slaves and others who were told they would be the slaves. But then, thank God, came Lincoln and Emancipation.

And before them, too, was a generation of Americans—the original native Americans—who watched the Mayflower *dock at Plymouth Rock. And I bet all the money in my pocket that they looked at those Pilgrims with their buckle shoes and said, "Man, America isn't what it used to be."*

The point is this: We have to spend less time worrying about how to make America what it was and more time worrying about making America what it will be.

That won't happen in one presidency. Or even in our lifetime. But we have to start now.

Shit Sandwiches

Of all the vulgarities and expletives in American politics, one of my favorites has to be "shit sandwich."

No, it's not the most popular curse among the political classes. It does not have the illustrious etymological history of, let's say, "Big f*cking deal." No vice president has ever been caught saying "shit sandwich" on a hot mike. Nor is there a record of Lyndon Johnson using it very often. And sailors cursed like *him*.

But I love "shit sandwich" anyway because the phrase is perfectly descriptive. It nails so many situations in Washington, where you're served bad deals that you've just got to scarf down no matter the nutritional value.

Up until now, though, "shit sandwich" has been only that—a metaphor. It's figurative. No politician wanted to actually give you two slices of Wonder Bread with a turd in between.

But then Senator Thom Tillis, a Republican from North Carolina, opened his mouth.

Speaking at the Bipartisan Policy Center in 2015, Tillis recalled a chat he'd had with a constituent at a Starbucks. The topic turned to regulation, as many chats with Republicans do, and Tillis was asked by the constituent about big government's intrusion into the bathroom at that very Starbucks—specifically, the sign, posted by law, requiring employees to wash their hands before returning to work.

This was a large . . . or, uh, venti . . . issue for Tillis. He believes that the government shouldn't be sticking its nose into any part of a private business. Not even the bathroom. And he said that he wouldn't "have any problem with Starbucks if they choose to opt out of this policy."[1]

What a capital idea, Mr. Tillis, I say! While we're at it, let's also allow Ford to sell cars without brakes. Or surgeons to perform operations while blindfolded. Or Coke to put real cocaine back in their soda pop. So long as it says so in the label's fine print. After all, Tillis's reasoning here is that markets are rational. If the public knows that Starbucks employees don't wash their hands, they can choose not to shop there, and the store will go out of business. As he says, "The market will take care of that."[2]

And maybe Tillis is right. Maybe the public would no-

tice there were no hand-washing-necessary signs at Starbucks. Maybe they'd say, "Ewww," and dash to the Dunkin'
Donuts across the street. Could happen. Hell, it probably
would happen.

But in the meantime, before word gets out about the
new bathroom policy at Starbucks, you can guess what else
is going to happen: One of those baristas is going to return
from doing his business, hands unwashed, and serve up an
adobo chicken panini with a little something extra on it.

Thom Tillis would give you a shit sandwich. Literally.

SENATOR TILLIS EVENTUALLY CLAIMED HE WAS ONLY
joking (which is what politicians always say after an inde-
fensible moronic statement). But joke or not, there was a
reason his hand-washing message became a headline and a
punchline: Republicans have been supporting antigovern-
ment political babble like this for years. They've constantly
said that government is too big, too burdensome, too intrusive. They've said that the market and the states should
be left alone. And they've meant it. Hell, the only kinds of
regulation conservatives *do* support are laws that say lesbi-
ans can't buy pizza—or bills that make a woman pay the
burial costs of her aborted fetus. *The government can regulate a uterus or a gay wedding, but nothing else.*

No one has summed up the conservative position here

as nicely as the antitax crusader Grover Norquist. He famously said that government should be so small that you could—and this is a direct quote—"drown it in a bathtub."

Call me crazy, but I have a different position on this. I'm not sure wanting to drown the government in a bathtub like an infanticidal babysitter is an ideal goal. On the contrary, sometimes government needs to do the babysitting. This is an opinion I've developed after the last twenty years of watching Republicans. They often need to be saved from their own idiocy.

Here's my favorite example: In February 2016 the GOP-dominated legislature in West Virginia deregulated the sale and consumption of unpasteurized dairy products. Previously, the government had prohibited raw milk sales for the small, simple reason that raw milk is often laced with bacteria and people can die after drinking it. "Milk sickness" is likely what killed Abraham Lincoln's stepmother. It's a primitive way to meet your maker. But then again, I suppose being a conservative means supporting the freedom to die unnecessarily like a nineteenth-century pioneer.

After the bill passed in West Virginia, legislators raised glasses of raw milk in celebration. "A lot of people haven't tasted raw milk," said one of the bill's supporters, "and they found out it's got a little better flavor than store-bought milk."[3]

Unfortunately, they also found out how raw milk tastes on the way back up their esophagi.

Soon after the celebratory drink, the lawmakers were rushing to the capitol toilets with all the symptoms of food poisoning, and it didn't take Louis Pasteur to figure out what was wrong. Republicans may have thought they'd use a bathroom to drown the government in the tub; instead, they ended up hunched over the toilet, puking out raw milk. (By the way, there's no word on whether they washed their hands before returning to work. Not that Senator Tillis would care.)

The reality is that the conservative obsession with deregulation doesn't make government work better. Or people safer. Or markets more efficient. Ask West Virginia.

Maybe the Republicans have been paying so much attention to the, ahem, anatomy of their presidential candidates that they're getting the wrong message: When it comes to government, *size doesn't matter.* Small government isn't always a good thing. It's not size, but smarts.

This is what Democrats have proven over the last twenty years again and again: Smart regulations and strong government can make a better country. As I wrote in 1996, "We need a federal government that is powerful enough to take on big business from time to time. We need a federal government that is powerful enough to protect the interests of the powerless."

On that score, we're still right. They're still wrong. And here's some more proof . . .

I WANT TO TALK A BIT ABOUT THREE OF THE MOST CONTEN-
tious debates over the role of government during the past
twenty years. Those would be Obamacare, Wall Street reform, and environmental regulations.

THOM TILLIS'S SIGNATURE CLUB SANDWICH

INGREDIENTS

- fresh turkey, sliced (I'm talking about turkey cut right off the bird, not deli meat)
- boiled ham, sliced thin
- I egg, fried
- 3 slices of thick-cut bacon, cooked crisp
- lettuce, tomato, onion
- three slices, sourdough bread
- spoonful of mayonnaise

DIRECTIONS

Spread mayonnaise on two of the bread slices. Assemble the sandwich as a triple-decker between the slices of sourdough bread, with the lettuce, tomato, onion, and the fried egg on top.

As an homage to Senator Tillis, feel free to include a dollop of spicy brown mustard to simulate the effect of eating in a restaurant without hand-washing regulations.

THANKS, OBAMA(CARE) ☺

In the alternate universe that exists inside a Tea Partier's cerebellum, America is a raging dumpster fire—and the thing that put the match to the garbage was, of course, Obamacare.

This has been the GOP party line for a while. Before the Affordable Care Act was even law, when it was still just a bill on Capitol Hill, the Republicans were peddling doom, predicting the demise of the United States. All because of some regulatory reforms to the health insurance market.

The GOP may have forgotten all the doom and gloom it has forecasted over the past eight years. But I haven't. So I've typed up a description of what America should look like today based on what Republicans themselves said. Everything between the quotation marks is quoted verbatim, and the wise conservative who said it is identified in parentheses after.

Without further ado, I present dispatches from the country formerly known as America in 2016:

**The United States once had a "very excellent
health care system," but it's gone now
[CARLY FIORINA].[4]**

Thanks to Obamacare, there is
"no insurance industry left"
(SENATOR TOM COBURN).[5]

Because of Obamacare, America is now
"bankrupt" and our economy is "ruined"
(THEN SPEAKER OF THE HOUSE JOHN BOEHNER).[6]

The health care law is
"America's biggest job-killer"
(SENATOR TED CRUZ).[7]

We have lost "about 2.5 million jobs"
and the deficit has increased "by $1 trillion"
(SENATOR LINDSEY GRAHAM).[8]

Today in America, "health care [is] unaffordable,"
and people "die sooner"
(SENATOR COBURN).[9]

Not only that, but Obamacare "literally kills women,
kills children, kills senior citizens"
(MICHELE BACHMANN).[10]

Bureaucrats determine "if you're going to
pull the plug on grandma"
(SENATOR CHUCK GRASSLEY).[11]

And babies with "Down syndrome . . . have to stand in
front of a 'death panel' so [Obama's] bureaucrats can
decide . . . whether they are worthy of health care"
**(EX-GOP VICE PRESIDENTIAL
CANDIDATE SARAH PALIN).**[12]

For those of us who remain alive, the law has been
"as destructive to personal and individual liberty
as the Fugitive Slave Act of 1850 that allowed
slave owners to . . . seize African Americans."
**(NEW HAMPSHIRE STATE
REPRESENTATIVE BILL O'BRIEN)**[13]

Congress now uses "the taxation power of the federal
government to compel behavior." There are "more
taxes if we don't drive Toyota Priuses or if we eat
too much junk food or . . . even [too little] pea soup."
America has a "new Gestapo—the IRS"
(MAINE GOVERNOR PAUL LePAGE).[14]

All right. Let's snap back to reality. Because anyone can
see that these visions of America are cuckoo for Cocoa
Puffs. None of those predictions came true. Last time I
checked, there aren't government doctors goose-stepping to
granny's house so they can pull the plug. We're not living

in a postapocalyptic America under the tyrannical thumb of big government health care. Quite the opposite.

Before I continue writing though, let me just give everyone a head's up . . .

WARNING! What you're about to read may cause spit takes and whiplash. Frequent Fox News watchers are advised to sit down and breathe deeply into a paper bag because everything you know about Obamacare is wrong.

The Affordable Care Act hasn't failed. In fact, it's a pretty damn successful piece of legislation, and I'll prove it.

In the '90s, I toyed around with a business idea. I wanted to scale up the squad of researchers and fact-checkers that had helped me debunk some of the most ridiculous GOP talking points of the 1992 campaign. I thought we could hire ourselves out to good liberals who would be trapped at backyard barbecues and cocktail parties debating politics with their Republican friends. We'd provide the facts in real time so our backyard clients could embarrass their neighbors. Then I'd collect my check.

For some reason, this business never got off the ground, but I still think it could be a useful public service, especially in the debate over Obamacare. Which is why, after twenty-five years of retirement, I'm bringing back *James Carville's Rapid Response Team*. Here's how we'd respond to some of the more ridiculous accusations about health care reform.

MYTH: Obamacare is a "job killer."

RAPID RESPONSE: Obamacare is a job killer like Ted Cruz is the Zodiac Killer. It's not true no matter how many times the Internet says it.

EXTENDED VERSION: The Affordable Care Act includes a provision called the "employer mandate," which says that companies employing more than fifty full-time employees are required to supply them with health insurance. This is the part of Obamacare that Republicans said would lead to layoffs, but as of this writing, it's been more than a year since the employer mandate kicked in, and the firings haven't happened.

Several studies say that Obamacare has had a "negligible" impact on the job market, and ADP, the nation's largest payroll company, has announced that there's no evidence of companies laying off workers or cutting their hours because of the health care mandate.[15] Also, let's not forget that 5.7 million private-sector jobs were created between January 2014, when the health care law went into full effect, and February 2016.[16]

Sometimes Republicans point to an old report from

the Congressional Budget Office that estimates Obamacare will reduce the amount of hours Americans work by 2024. Republicans say this means 2.5 million people will be fired, but it's actually the opposite.[17] It means more people will be able to quit, to leave a job when they want to. Maybe because they don't have to rely on their employer for health insurance.

Here's the director of the Congressional Budget Office, Douglas Elmendorf, testifying before Congress:

> *The reason that we don't use the term "lost jobs" is there's a critical difference between people who would like to work and can't find a job or have a job that is lost for reasons beyond their control and people who choose not to work.*
>
> *If somebody comes to you and says, "I've decided to retire or I've decided to stay home and spend more time with my family," . . . [then w]e say congratulations. And we don't say they've lost their job because they have chosen to leave that job.[18]*

MYTH: Obamacare is an affront to individual liberty and opens the door to more taxation on SUVs and junk food. It's the "New Gestapo."

RAPID RESPONSE: Really? Do I have to dignify this with a response?

EXTENDED RESPONSE: I'm just going to ignore this and go pick up a Snickers bar in my Ford F-150, neither of which I am being taxed extra for.

MYTH: "Obamacare is not helping . . . the families it was intended to help."—*Carly Fiorina*

RAPID RESPONSE:

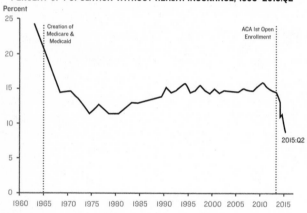

PERCENT OF POPULATION WITHOUT HEALTH INSURANCE, 1963-2015:Q2

In the words of George Tenet, the CIA director who claimed Iraq had WMDs, this is a "slam dunk"— except this time it actually is.

Obamacare was intended to help the families of the 46 million people who didn't have and couldn't afford health insurance. In 2016 alone, 12.7 million people have signed up on the exchanges that Obamacare established. In total, 20 million more Americans have health insurance.[19]

EXTENDED RESPONSE: Let's see how these numbers compare to life before Obamacare.

Since people started enrolling on health care exchanges in 2014, the percent of uninsured people in America has dropped more than 5 percent. In 2015 one study from the CDC found that the uninsured rate had dropped below 10 percent, the first time that has happened in American history.[20]

MYTH: "There will be no insurance industry left . . . [Obamacare is] going to make insurance unaffordable for everyone—which is what they want. Because if there's no private insurance left, what's left? Government-centered, government-run, single-payer health care."—*Senator Tom Coburn, October 2010*

RAPID RESPONSE: Maybe Senator Coburn's office didn't compile his news clips during Christmas week of 2015. It would be understandable. But it would've also meant the senator missed the following news, which broke that week.

In 2015 sign-ups on the Obamacare exchanges accelerated more than the prior year's rate, up 29 percent. This unexpected spike in sign-ups drove hospital stocks higher during a period when the health insurance industry had seen favorable stock market results, too.[21] The country's top five insurers have beaten the S&P 500 every year since Obamacare's ratification.[22]

I'm no expert but it seems to me that (1) when more people buy health insurance, it probably means it's more affordable and (2) if stock prices go up, too, it probably means the private sector is doing just fine.

EXTENDED RESPONSE: I'll unpack Senator Coburn's argument a bit more. His belief was that Obamacare would blow up the health insurance industry by driving premiums so high that no one would want to be a customer. Then the government would be forced to step in and build its own socialist health care system over the burning ruin of the old private system.

It's a neat conspiracy theory, and like most conspiracy theories, it's also 100 percent BS. Not only is the private insurance industry alive and well, health care prices are also more affordable. Premiums rose slower than they had in previous years. In fact, even for people who didn't qualify for discounts or government subsidies, health care premiums went up by 8 percent in 2015. Compare that to the 10-plus percent increases usually seen in the decade before Obamacare's passage.[23]

MYTH: Obamacare "literally kills our women, our children, our senior citizens."

RAPID RESPONSE: If you believe Obamacare is killing people, why don't you just click out of your Internet browser—where I also assume you're looking at 9/11 truther videos—and google "Brent Brown" instead.

EXTENDED RESPONSE: Brent Brown is a Republican voter from Wisconsin who used to call President Obama a "liar who betrayed America." Not long after Obamacare was passed, Brent was diagnosed with a serious bowel condition.[24] He wrote a letter to President Obama explaining what happened next. Brent wrote:

> *I did not vote for you. Either time. I have voted Republican for the entirety of my life. I proudly wore pins and planted banners displaying my Republican loyalty. I was very vocal in my opposition to you— particularly the ACA. Before I briefly explain my story allow me to first say this: I am so very sorry. I was so very wrong.*
>
> *You saved my life. My President, you saved my life, and I am eternally grateful.*

> *I have a "pre-existing condition" and so could never purchase health insurance. Only after the ACA came into being could I be covered. Put simply . . . I would not be alive without access to care I received due to your law.*[25]

Thanks, Obama(care).

A MODEST GUN PROPOSAL FOR REPUBLICANS

When I debate gun control with one of Mary's conservative friends, things always get heated. There's no way to avoid that. Regulating Second Amendment rights is a hot-trigger issue.

I realize now that it's not very wise to start a yelling match with someone who might be concealing and carrying. So in the interest of self-preservation, I'll cede the whole debate right now. I, James Carville, will admit that Democrats are wrong on guns. We should have Glocks without background checks. Uzis for middle schoolers. Grenade launchers in the sale bin at Best Buy. I'll allow all of it.

But the Republicans have to do one thing first.

They have to let everyone bring their guns to the Republican National Convention in 2020.

Guns were prohibited at the 2016 convention in Cleveland, which is strange to me because a convention floor seems like the next logical place to expand gun rights, a sort of manifest destiny for the Second Amendment. Republicans have already voted for your right to carry in all sorts of public places: churches in Georgia . . . state parks in Maine, Louisiana, and Virginia . . . stadiums, hospitals, and day care centers in Michigan . . . Mississippi high schools, courthouses, polling places, colleges, churches, and the passenger terminal of Jackson-Evers International Airport in Mississippi.[26]

Thanks to Republican legislators, you'll soon be able to pack heat on the quad of Texas A&M or at the college bar in town. Which brings a whole new meaning to "taking a shot."[27]

But for some reason, the march of progress hasn't made it yet to political rallies. When the RNC chose the spot for the 2016 convention, they selected Quicken Loans Arena in Cleveland, where a stadium policy "strictly" forbids firearms. The arena refused to budge even after a petition was circulated calling for the convention to be a "gun-friendly zone."[28] (The Secret Service said they'd prohibit firearms, too.)

This has to be an oversight. You see, the conservative argument against gun-free zones—and for the right to carry anywhere—is that it deters gun violence. And if it doesn't deter gun violence, then at least it gives anybody the chance to put two in the chest of a wannabe murderer. As Ted Cruz put it, "You stop bad guys by using our guns."[29]

Cruz wasn't alone here; conservatives haven't been shy about this. After the attacks in Paris, Donald Trump said that had the victims been carrying it would have been a "much, much different situation."[30] Then Ben Carson shared this interesting bit of history: Jews might have prevented the Holocaust if they'd been packing heat in the ghettos.[31] In other words, guns don't kill people. *Guns just kill people who don't have guns.*

This is why it's crazy that the Republican National Convention didn't declare itself a "gun-friendly zone" no matter what the stadium or the Secret Service agents said. Republicans knew they needed to protect themselves. The RNC boss, Reince Priebus, should've put out a press release, a thumbs-up next to a trigger finger, demanding that

Quicken Loans Arena reverse its policy. And Ohio governor John Kasich and his Republican legislature should've suspended the pesky law that allows the arena to set its antigun policy. That way, the Second Amendment could've been in the speeches—*and in the waistbands*—of everyone at the convention.

After all, these big political conventions always attract their fair share of threats. And sure, the Secret Service is there with snipers to protect the nominee. But shouldn't the Republicans on the floor—the guys from the Sacramento Chamber of Commerce and the fellows of the Heritage Foundation—be able to lock and load if ISIS breaks through the security barrier?

Or what about outside of the arena? I don't know where the next election cycle's convention will be held, but if it's anything like Cleveland, guns will be a priority. After all, Cleveland is so *urrrrban*. It's full of . . . How do I put this gently? What's the euphemism Republicans would use? . . . *Cleveland is full of Democrats.* And when you're feeling threatened in a city you don't know, you need protection. As the failed Senate candidate Sharron Angle reminded us, Republicans should be ready with "Second Amendment remedies" should a threat ever pop up.

And if the threat never comes? Well . . . at least the conventiongoers can take some target practice when the balloons drop. There's nothing more fun than some .22-caliber fireworks.

Someone should just warn the nominee about the ricochet.

LET ME BE (DODD-)FRANK

Meet Jeb Hensarling—the other Jeb of the Republican Party.

Mr. Hensarling is a fellow you should know. He's a congressman from Texas, an endorser of Ted Cruz for president, and a former Eagle Scout. But more important than all that, Jeb churns out some of the GOP's best talking points when it comes to Wall Street.

Jeb is the chairman of the House Financial Services Committee, the congressional body that has overseen all of the House's efforts to reform Wall Street, including, once upon a time, the Dodd-Frank Act.

You might be familiar with Dodd-Frank. Congress

passed the law back in 2010, almost three years after risky trading sent America's financial sector into a tailspin and nearly toppled the big banks. Dodd-Frank's aim was—and is—to prevent this from happening again, to stop the big banks from engaging in risky trading, and to make sure that, if another crisis hits, the banks could go out of business without taking the economy with them.

Much like every bill inked with President Obama's signature, Dodd-Frank is hated by Republicans. But none hate it quite as much as Mr. Hensarling. "I will not rest," Jeb has said, "until Dodd-Frank is ripped out by its roots and tossed on the trash heap of history."[32]

This is weak sauce compared to Jeb's usual critique of Dodd-Frank. He has called the law:

- a "monument to the arrogance and hubris of man"
- "bureaucratic tyranny [that] would make a Soviet commissar blush"
- and, of course, "regulatory waterboarding"

Typically, I'd have to search through years of transcripts to find quotes like that, but Jeb was creative enough to fit those lines in the same speech—a speech from March 2016 in which he also quotes Ronald Reagan, Teddy Roosevelt, Paul Ryan, Bono, and Kanye West. (Apparently, Jeb believes that America's leading rapper is a fan of unregulated credit-default swaps.)[33]

Anyway, Jeb's recent speech is a remarkable document, real A+ stuff. But for my money, his best material came back in 2011, when Jeb was just the lowly vice chairman of the Financial Services Committee. Because that's when he and the chairman, Spencer Bachus of Alabama, published a pamphlet about all the terrible things Dodd-Frank would do to the country. They made all sorts of predictions.

You'd think Republicans would know not to make doomsday forecasts by now. You'd think they would've learned from the Obamacare debate or even the president's promise that the stimulus would keep the unemployment rate under 8 percent. But no. Jeb and Spencer published their predictions—and they actually called them "predictions"—which read like a parade of horribles that Dodd-Frank would unleash on the nation.

Five years later, I thought it might be fun to see how those predictions hold up.

PREDICTION, 2011: "Unilateral adoption of the Volcker rule [the rule that stops big banks from engaging in risky trading] will only undermine our competitive advantage, in my opinion, and therefore is going to undermine the profitability of financial institutions."—*Spencer Bachus*[34]

REALITY, 2016: Has Dodd-Frank hurt Wall Street's bottom line? Oh, no! It looks like Bachus may have a point. In 2015, the average Wall Street bonus check was *ONLY $146,000!!!!*

In all seriousness, I have no problem with people earning good money. Hell, I make a pretty good living myself. But what I can't stand is the claim that regulation is grievously harming the financial industry. In 2014 banks recorded $40.24 billion in profits, the second highest amount since data have been collected on the subject.[35] Nor has regulation hurt investors. The Dow Jones Industrial Average went up almost 80 percent between July 2010 and April 2016.[36]

PREDICTION, 2011: "[Dodd-Frank will raise] the cost of capital to American businesses, consumers, and home buyers, and it will slow economic activity and job creation."
—*Spencer Bachus*

"Why would we enact any legislation that would harm the ability of small businesses to access credit in the midst of a credit contraction?"—*Jeb Hensarling*

REALITY, 2016: At the core of these predictions is the argument that Dodd-Frank slows lending at small banks, which are largely responsible for lending to local small businesses and home buyers.

It's true that the number of small community banks, like the kind where George Bailey worked in *It's a Wonderful Life*, has declined. But (1) this trend has been happening since the early '90s, and (2) a smaller number of banks doesn't mean a smaller number of loans. In fact, loan balances at community banks are now growing twice as fast as the balances at big banks, according to FDIC data. Loan growth at small banks has outpaced the bigger banks since early 2015.[37]

As for home buyers? Well, it's also true that Dodd-Frank has made it harder for people to get home loans. BUT THAT WAS THE POINT OF THE LAW!

Risky mortgages were one of the main drivers of the financial crisis, and "substantially diminishing the number of loans that are made for residential mortgages that should not have been made was the single biggest thing we did," says Barney Frank, the former Democratic congressman and co-namesake of the law.[38]

PREDICTION, 2011: Dodd-Frank is "going to lead to greater volatility in food and energy prices, and a loss of capital investments."—*Spencer Bachus*

REALITY, 2016: Let's tell the truth here, Mr. Bachus. Food prices were spiking long before Dodd-Frank. Like the extinction of small banks, this has been happening since the '90s, and it has little to do with financial regulations. In fact, a lot of the experts think that a *deregulated* market is what leads to food price volatility. That's because big investors are able to drive up the price of commodities like wheat.[39]

People are making money off hunger, and this is something Dodd-Frank tried to stop by preventing the world's food supply from falling into the hands of just a few investors.

As for gas prices? Well, those have been reliably going in one direction for the last six years—down, waaaaaay down. When you adjust for inflation, the price of a gallon of gas in 2015 was only seven cents higher than it was in 1929![40]

HERE ARE MY FINAL THOUGHTS ON DODD-FRANK AND CON-gressman Hensarling: The man should be very thankful he went into politics and not fortune-telling. Otherwise, he'd be one of those belly-up small businesses he so often talks about.

Jeb and Co.'s success rate for predicting the outcome of Dodd-Frank has been close to nil. To hear him tell it, Lower Manhattan should be a ghost town right now. America should be storing its money under the mattress. Dodd-Frank didn't lead to any of that.

Does this mean that the law is beyond criticism? No, sir. No, ma'am. Of course not. Any 2,000-plus-page piece of legislation is going to have glitches and unintended consequences, and Dodd-Frank certainly has its share. Small banks, for example, are having a hard time jumping through extra regulatory hoops because, unlike large banks, they don't have the budgets to hire more lawyers. Even worse, regulators have found that, as of last spring, five of the country's biggest banks still haven't devised reliable strategies to shut their doors without tanking the economy.[41] Some financial institutions are likely still too big to fail, but that's a reason to improve banking regulations, not "rip them out by the roots and toss them on the trash heap of history."

The God's honest truth, though, is this: Of course, laws like Dodd-Frank have their downside. That's the point. Wall Street reform was always going to make life more difficult for bankers and loans more scarce for low-credit home buyers, because with those costs came a big benefit—like decreasing the risk of another financial crisis. Every regulation is a trade-off.

Jeb Hensarling may quote from Bono and Kanye West to support his case, but I have the Father of Economics, Adam Smith, on my side. In 1776, the same year that

America declared her independence, Smith wrote that "regulations may, no doubt, be considered as in some respects a violation of natural liberty. But those exertions of the natural liberty of a few individuals, which might endanger the security of a whole society, are, and ought to be, restrained by the laws of all governments."

Smith then went on to compare banking regulations to the walls that, say, a housing code might mandate to prevent the spread of fire. "The obligation of building party walls, in order to prevent the communication of fire," he said, "is a violation of natural liberty exactly of the same kind with the regulations of the banking trade which are here proposed."[42]

In other words, it's natural to hate regulation until you're caught in a firestorm. Then you'll thank God for it.

GREEN LAWS AND BROWN WATER

A message to small government extremists: If you think environmental regulations are unnecessary and burdensome, why don't you put your mouth where your mouth is?

Go to Flint, Michigan, and touch your lips to a tall glass of tap water.

In 2014 Flint's water began flowing out of the tap the color of shit, with high levels of chloride, fecal coliform, and lead. General Motors had reported that the same water was corroding car parts at a facility nearby. Yet, for more than a year, state officials told people it was safe to drink.

Flash forward to today; doctors now estimate that there are upward of 8,000 children—many of them poor and black—who have *way* too much lead in their blood. It's a condition that leads to learning disabilities, motor-skill problems, and even violent behavior. We still don't know what the long-term effects will be.[43]

How did Flint end up drinking poison? Well, under the Safe Drinking Water Act, the Environmental Protection Agency—the EPA—sets the standards for tap water. But it's up to the states to implement those standards. And Flint's crisis began when the state-appointed city manager decided to switch Flint's water source. The city started siphoning their H_2O from the polluted Flint River.[44]

When someone writes the book on Flint—and they probably already are—America will have to reckon with a series of actions as disgusting as the Flint water itself. For example, Flint looked for a different, cheaper water supply because Republicans in the governor's mansion and the legislature had been pressuring the city to cut costs.

It's also hard to dispute that this was an act of environmental racism—and, yes, "racism" is the right word. Could you imagine this happening in Greenwich, Connecticut, or Jupiter, Florida, and not a poor black city? I can't. But if something like that did happen, you know that the people who poisoned kids just to save a buck would be wearing orange jumpsuits by now.

That said, what's pissed me off most has been the Republican response to all this, the idea that Flint is proof that environmental regulations do not work. Here's Donald Trump talking about Flint: "Environmental protection—we waste all of this money," he says. "We're going to bring that back to the states."[45] (I have a question for you, Donald: Is that orange hair dye seeping into your brain? Or are you drinking the water in Flint, too? Because giving power to the states—particularly the state of Michigan—is what caused this whole crisis.)

Look, I'm fine with conservatives casting blame on whomever here. As far as I'm concerned, the brown water is on everyone's hands, from the governor, Rick Snyder, up to the feds at the EPA. The law may not have given the EPA the power it needed, but people with lead poisoning don't really care about excuses. They care about fixing the damn problem.

Trump's idea for gutting the EPA wouldn't fix Flint's problem, though. Not even a little bit. Nor would it prevent such a crisis from happening again. It would do the opposite. Gutting the EPA after Flint would be like shooting your guard dog for not stopping a robbery—even though you'd tied the dog to a tree beforehand. The solution isn't to kill the dog. It's to let Fido off the leash.

Strong environmental regulations have a pretty good track record in this country. It turns out that when we untether the guard dogs they do more than just bark. One of the best examples is banning lead in gasoline, which the federal government first took steps to do in 1973. Back then, the lead in gasoline fumes, a lot like the lead in Flint's water, produced a range of health and developmental problems. The worst affected were poor and minority kids in the inner city, where street congestion was highest. The Centers for Disease Control and Prevention estimated that in the late 1970s, almost 90 percent of American children aged one through five had enough lead in their blood to merit the term "level of concern." Today, because of the restrictions on lead in gasoline, less than 1 percent do.[46]

Another great example is the effort to reduce air pollution. Under President Obama, the EPA rolled out a Clean Power Plan in 2015 that was aimed at reducing pollution and carbon emissions, especially from coal-fired power plants over the next fifteen years. Researchers from Harvard and Syracuse University independently confirmed that by 2030 the measure would prevent up to 3,600 premature deaths, 90,000 asthma attacks in children, 1,700 heart attacks, and 300,000 missed days of school and work.[47]

You can also see the success of activist government when it comes to the issue affecting Flint: clean water. In fact, twenty years ago, when I wrote *We're Right, They're Wrong*, the big debate was over the Clean Water Act. Back then the chief critic of environmental regulations was the House Republican majority leader, Tom DeLay. Today Tom is best known to some voters for his mug shot, where he's smiling like a jackass after being arrested for corruption. (His conviction was later overturned on appeal.) But in the '90s, DeLay was best known for comparing laws that protected rivers to the Gestapo. (Is it just me, or are Republicans running out of Nazi-related metaphors?)

Well, after twenty years, the verdict is in for Tom—not on the corruption charges, but on his idea that the government shouldn't be involved in ensuring clean water. Two health economists, David Cutler and Grant Miller, released a landmark study in which they determined the reason for the large increase in Americans' life expectancy at the beginning of the twentieth century. "Half of the dramatic decline in mortality between 1900 and 1936—a period in which life expectancy increased from less than 50 years to more than 60—was due *just to improved municipal water systems*," they said.

Since then, laws at the federal level have served to only improve our water supply. In fact, the Clean Water Act, which Tom DeLay did not like one bit, helped purify the Great Lakes, the original source of Flint's water before the city manager switched to the river.[48]

This brings me to one last note about Flint: Obviously the government has to do better to protect people. But in this case, better does not mean less. It means government must do more. Energetic government has prevented and fixed crises like Flint before. It must do it again.

Otherwise, America will eat shit. Literally.

BEFORE WE MOVE ON, I WANT TO ADDRESS THE ONE OTHER big myth about environmental laws—that they hurt the economy.

Republicans love spewing this crap. It's a neat little narrative they spin, that we Democrats are tree huggers, that we'd rather disrupt business and fire blue-collar workers than disturb the habitat of the woolly owl or the yellow-spotted salamander or whatever.

Well, let's set aside the fact that yellow-spotted salamanders probably have higher IQs than most conservative legislators. None of what the Republicans say is true. In fact, it's the opposite of true. Environmental regulations aren't job killers. They're job savers, an economic firewall.

Here's where my thinking originates from: One of my oldest buddies, Cyril Vetter, recently produced a documentary called *After the Spill*. It's about how the 2010 BP oil spill devastated the Louisiana coastline and how we should regulate the oil industry in the aftermath. Cyril was kind enough to send a camera to my house and film my thoughts on the matter.

The oil industry has always maintained a friendly relationship with Louisiana regulators. And I mean "friendly" in the biblical sense. According to a state inspector general's report, regulators were "having sexual relationships with oil and gas company representatives" before the spill. They also "frequently consumed alcohol at industry functions, [and] had used cocaine and marijuana." (It sounds like Grover Norquist isn't the only one trying to relive the '80s.)[49]

Nevertheless, a group of Louisiana politicos wanted to overlook the general incompetence. They wanted to keep the reins loose on the oil industry even after the spill. Their argument boiled down to this: The oil industry has been good to Louisiana. The industry has created jobs, generated revenue, and, best of all, filled the campaign coffers of state politicians. Why punish the oil industry, they say, and force the drilling platforms and thousands of jobs to go elsewhere?

When Cyril's interviewer asked for my response, I went for the laugh line: I said that I feel the same way about the oil industry as I do about the Catholic Church. After all, the Catholic Church does a lot of good, too, feeding the hungry and healing the sick. But that doesn't mean that

Father O'Malley can touch the altar boy and get away with it. BP can't get away with it either, I said.

In retrospect, I shouldn't have gone for the laugh, however. *I should have gone for the jugular.* Because the premise of the question was bogus. Who says a deregulated oil industry creates more jobs? Sure, it may create jobs at companies like BP or Exxon or Shell. But what about the jobs at the Gulf Coast hotels or on the shrimping boats or at the restaurants? One study found that the oil spill cost 22,000 people their jobs, and that study was limited to industries that rely only on fishing.[50] A deregulated oil industry killed those jobs. A regulated industry may have saved them.

I'm not just talking about clean water and healthy fish, though. I'm talking about a clean environment across the board. All of that protects the economy. An example: In 1970, Congress passed the Clean Air Act to stop industry from spewing pollution into the sky, and ever since, companies have paid a pretty penny to comply with the law. According to the EPA, the country's annual cost of compliance will reach about $65 billion a year by 2020.

But as big as those costs are, the benefits of clean air are so much bigger. Over the past fifty years, the Clean Air Act has been responsible for a dramatic improvement in public health, including a one-to-two-year increase in the average American's life expectancy. By the end of the decade, the

EPA estimates that clean air regulations will save 17.4 million lost workdays and will also prevent 230,000 adults from dying too early every year. All of this translates into an annual economic benefit of two trillion dollars—or more than thirty times the cost of compliance.[51]

Still believe that environmental regulations hurt the economy? I'll give you another example: A few years back, *The Washington Post* reported on a coal-fired power plant on the Muskingum River in Ohio. Because of EPA rules, AEP, the company that runs the plant, had to shut it down in 2014, sooner than it would have liked. Around 160 jobs were lost.

But that's not the end of the story. Because, thanks to

incentives from the Obama administration, AEP opened up a new clean-burning natural-gas plant an hour's drive north from the old one. Building that plant created hundreds of jobs, and it will employ twenty-five people full-time.

"Some jobs are lost. Others are created," wrote the *Post*'s reporter. "In the end, say economists who have studied this question, the overall impact on employment is minimal."[52]

The data bears this out. In fact, the U.S. Bureau of Labor and Statistics used to compile a list of all things that kill jobs, and regulation ranked at almost the very bottom. In the first quarter of 2013, only one half of 1 percent of all mass-layoff events were due to "government regulations/ intervention." For comparison: There were six times as many mass layoffs the quarter before due to "extreme weather" like Hurricane Sandy.* And when was the last time you heard the GOP call climate change a "job killer"? You haven't.[53]

Republicans don't seem to grasp this. The only jobs that matter to them, it seems, are at the companies deserving regulation—polluters and oil companies, big banks and health insurance firms. They don't see that, overall, regula-

---

* By the way, there's a reason those statistics are out of date.

In 2013, when the Republicans couldn't come to a budget deal and forced the sequester, there were deep government spending cuts. The U.S. Bureau of Labor and Statistics had to shut down their mass-layoff data collection program.

A little coincidental, huh? The GOP got rid of the data that proved their point.

tion doesn't kill jobs; it just transfers them to industries that are cleaner, safer, and better for the country.

CRAWFISH MONGERS

In a lot of ways, the lesson of this chapter reminds me of one of my earliest memories. It's a story I first told in my book *Had Enough?*, but it seems too fitting to skip over here.

Back when I was a kid, I'd go with my momma and grandma to a place called Pierre Part to buy crawfish. The men working the little stand out by the dock were courteous to my momma and grandma and would talk about how they were going to give us a good price on the best catch and how well we'd be eating that night. Then they'd start talking to each other in French about how they were going to rip us off.

Well, the men didn't realize that my mother and my grandma both spoke French—and the minute they heard what those dockhands were saying, they called them out on it. In French, my momma said something to the effect of "Ain't gonna happen, boys."

When it comes to the proper role of government, Republicans are like those dockhands selling crawfish. They're trying to pull a fast one on the country. They tell Americans that regulations—whether they're meant to reform health care or to rein in Wall Street or to protect the environment—are all job killers. And then, in a language not everyone understands—the language of hard-core conservative ideologues—Republicans admit the truth. They admit that they're not really interested in improving the country, just in protecting their big-business donors and in advancing their small-government, let-the-market-run-wild view of the world.

Twenty years ago, when I wrote the original version of this book, I took a swing at Phil Gramm, the then Republican senator from Texas, who was very loud in espousing his small-government ideology. "The market is rational and the government is dumb," Gramm said. I didn't think serious people could still believe that after a deregulated financial industry helped put us in a worldwide recession, and yet at Washington gatherings, we still hear variations on this theme from people like Senator Thom Tillis and Donald Trump.

The truth is: Republicans don't really care if deregulation means a crashed economy or that more Americans will drink brown water. After all, the GOP has already imbibed something much more toxic.

They've drunk the Kool-Aid of small government extremism.

The Anatomy of Bullshit

Maybe it was growing up in the Mississippi River mud, which will steal your shoes if you step in it, but I've grown accustomed to getting stuck in strange places. There was that offshore dredger where I was a deckhand; a couple of New Orleans bars with various men and women of disrepute; and every time Mary hosts a fund-raiser, I'm besieged by someone talking about building a border wall. Also, for most weeknights during the past decade, I was contractually obligated to sit and have Republicans yell at me on national television.

Anyway, none of these are even close to the weirdest place an American has been held against their will.

By far, that was a plastic tent in the parking garage of a Newark, New Jersey, hospital. The tent was small, with just a hospital bed and a box for a toilet. No shower. No heat.

Its sole occupant was Ms. Kaci Hickox of South Portland, Maine.

Ms. Hickox wasn't imprisoned in the tent because she was in trouble. She wasn't a bank robber or a horse thief. She wasn't smuggling maple syrup, which I assume accounts for most of the crime in Maine. And even though her food was delivered by hospital workers, who carefully dropped the meals through a plastic window cut in the front, Kaci was not there because she was sick. She *wasn't* sick.

Ms. Hickox was there for one reason only, and it probably smelled a lot like the stench wafting out of that box toilet.

Kaci was there because of bullshit.

Bullshit is the subject of this chapter, and I define it as the following:

> **bullshit** /*būl-shit*/ **noun**—a fake crisis or scandal manufactured by politicians to exploit, for political purposes, the fear and anger of the American public (e.g., "Kaci Hickox was imprisoned because of bullshit").

In the autumn of 2014, Ms. Hickox—a nurse—spent a month in the West African country of Sierra Leone caring for people infected in the widespread Ebola outbreak. Now, unless you are fatally allergic to cable news—and I know some people who say they are—you remember Ebola. It's a nightmare disease, a bad, bad way to go. And in West Africa, people were dying, more than 11,000 of them in 2014.[1]

In the United States, the story was different.

When Kaci flew home in October of that year, only one person had died of Ebola in the United States. That person had not contracted the disease in America; he was infected abroad and then flew to Dallas. There were also two health care workers who'd caught the disease while treating the Dallas man and two others—a doctor and a cameraman— who were infected in Africa. But all four of those folks were on their way to full recoveries.

Only 0.000002 percent of the American population was infected with Ebola in late 2014. No one who had caught Ebola here ever died. And the two people who caught Ebola here were cured in a couple of weeks' time. In a sound bite, while there were individual cases of Ebola in the fall of 2014, there was no Ebola outbreak.[2]

Let me tap the microphone and repeat that again: *There was no Ebola outbreak in the United States.*

Now, it's understandable if that's not the version of the story you remember. I get it. Based on the cable coverage, America in the time of Ebola was a vast infectious waste- land. We were on our way to total societal collapse, to being ruled by roving bands of motorcycle warlords who used human teeth as currency. (Okay. Maybe I exaggerate. But the fear was real. The stock market crashed. Schools closed. There was a run on protective medical supplies: gloves, sanitizer, those little white masks you pull over your mouth.)[3]

Who was stoking this fear?

Well, it wasn't the medical community. They'd been up front from the beginning. In August, more than a month before America had its first Ebola diagnosis, the Centers for Disease Control and Prevention predicted exactly what was going to happen. Based on the spread of Ebola in Africa—and the fact that international air travel exists—they said it was "inevitable" that someone with Ebola would eventually come to America. In fact, one model showed that there was an 18 percent chance of an Ebola case as soon as October 1. The first case was confirmed on September 30.[4]

(Side note: No one got shorter shrift during this whole ordeal than the medical community. Weathermen can barely predict that it's going to rain three days out, and no one gives them a hard time. Our doctors nailed Ebola a month in advance, and still people said there was no warning.)

But while doctors said that Ebola in the United States was inevitable, they also said that it wasn't a cause for fear. "We are confident that there will not be a large Ebola outbreak in the U.S.," Tom Frieden, the head of the CDC, told Congress, and he was right.[5] After all, Ebola is very difficult to catch. Unlike the flu, it isn't airborne. It spreads through the bodily fluids of people who are symptomatic— or already dead. So unless you were swapping spit with a corpse or sticking yourself with the needles used to treat Ebola patients, you were likely fine.

In 2014 experts weren't even recommending travel bans to Africa or mandatory quarantines for folks who'd been there. This, they said, would actually make the problem worse by deterring health care workers from traveling to Africa and treating the pandemic at its origin. The doctors were advising vigilance, not panic.[6] Unfortunately, certain people who run the country were advising the exact opposite.

Republicans encouraged America to lose its collective shit.

From the very first news stories—when we were only bringing back infected American aid workers to be cared for in modern hospitals—politicians, almost all Republican, fueled the flames of panic. Donald Trump (of course) was the first out of the gate, saying we should leave all Ebola victims, even American aid workers, to die in Africa.[7] But once we had one confirmed case of Ebola in America, the floodgates opened. Senator Rand Paul accused the president of lying about the outbreak.[8] And Congressman Peter

King, a member of the Select Committee on Intelligence, wondered if the "strain had mutated" and was now "airborne," which I think is just a line from that old Dustin Hoffman movie *Outbreak.*[9]

And let's not overlook the typical conservative trolls like Todd Kincannon, the former head of the South Carolina Republican Party. The man does with bigotry what Michelangelo did with marble, and he did some of his best work with this Twitter rant:

Todd Kincannon
@toddkincannon

People with Ebola in the US need to be humanely put down immediately.

The protocol for a positive Ebola test should be immediate humane and execution and sanitization of the whole area. That will save lives.

The people of Africa are to blame for why it's so shitty. They could stop eating each other and learn calculus at any time.

There's just no other way with Ebola. We need to be napalming villages from the air right now.[10]

Kudos to you, Todd! Unfortunately, you lose first place in the crazy contest to Chris Christie; he was the first to turn the panic into policy.

The New Jersey governor (and unsuccessful presidential contender) has a knack for holding press conferences that, in retrospect, are carnivals. Will anyone forget the day when he spent 108 minutes at a press conference denying he'd caused a traffic jam on the George Washington Bridge to punish a political enemy?

But among Christie's greatest hits is the media session he held in late October 2014 to announce a new Ebola policy. He was joined by Governor Andrew Cuomo of New York. (It pains me to say that Democrats like Cuomo were complicit in this, but some were.) Christie and Cuomo said that if any aid workers returned from helping Ebola victims in Africa and flew into one of the airports in their states, they'd be placed under a "mandatory quarantine" for three weeks.

Where did they come up with this policy? No idea. Again, the people with actual medical degrees didn't recommend this. Everyone from the United Nations to the CDC came out against it.[11]

Best guess: Christie and Cuomo pulled this policy out of their asses.

Which brings us back to Kaci Hickox and the Ebola tent. When Kaci flew into New Jersey—and walked through Newark International Airport—this was the situation she entered. She had her temperature taken with a forehead scanner, a machine that's often wrong. It said she had a slight fever, something not all that uncommon after a day of international air travel crammed into coach. All the subsequent thermometers said Kaci was fine, but it didn't matter. She was whisked off to the parking lot of Rutgers University Hospital, where she was forced inside a tent for forty-eight hours.

The only time she ever heard from Chris Christie was through her mother, who'd seen the New Jersey governor speak on television. He'd told reporters and the world that Kaci clearly had Ebola, that she was "obviously ill."[12]

But Christie wasn't a doctor. And he'd never seen Kaci. He was too busy on the campaign trail in Florida.

THE GREAT EBOLA PANIC OF 2014 WASN'T THE FIRST BULLSHIT crisis in American history. Far from it. American history is full of bullshit. Politicians have been stoking fear and conjuring up fake catastrophes since Thomas Jefferson accused John Adams of trying to marry his son off to King George's daughter so they could start a new American monarchy. Adams claimed a Jefferson presidency would lead to "children writhing on a pike."[13]

As recently as the 1980s, the Religious Right was spreading the myth that devil worshippers were kidnapping babies and taking them to the woods for use in evil rituals. Historians dubbed it the Great Satanic Panic. (And, yes, this happened in the 1980s, not the 1680s.)[14]

Today we see these chapters in history as absurd. We laugh at them. They're random trivia, *Jeopardy!* questions and podcast episodes. But more and more often, we're also caught up in new versions of these panics. The worst parts of history repeat themselves. And we don't notice. Or if we do notice, we're not good enough at dismissing the bullshit.

Why is this happening? Maybe it's the rise of cable news and Internet lunacy—there's more room for crazy voices. Maybe it's that the crazy voices are welcomed on air. Or maybe we're far enough removed from the granddaddy of all bullshit political panics—McCarthyism and the witch hunt for communists in the 1950s—that we forget our politicians, especially Republicans, are good at making shit up.

In the end, it doesn't matter why it happens. Shit happens. And so does bullshit. Indeed, the only thing that matters about bullshit—and I come by this lesson after years in rural Louisiana—is that you have to avoid stepping in it.

So I want to give you a crash course in how to avoid planting your foot in bullshit and how you can teach others to do the same. Let's put three of the biggest bullshit crises of the past twenty years on the examination table. Unlike Chris Christie, I will admit that I am no doctor. But after a

half century in politics, bullshit is the one disease I can diagnose.

Let me present my medical lecture, "The Anatomy of
Bullshit: Three Lessons in Sniffing Out Political Panics,"
sponsored by the Republican Party, with additional support from your friends in cable news.

> **LESSON 1** If the People Telling You to Panic
> Also Happen to Benefit from That
> Panic . . . IT'S BULLSHIT!

If you look closely, America's Ebola panic did not begin on
September 30, 2014, when the country's first case of the
disease was diagnosed in Dallas. Nor did it start on October 24 when Christie and Cuomo held their joint press
conference. Nor two days later when Kaci Hickox was
pulled out of the terminal in Newark-Liberty International
Airport.

The day that determined if there'd be an Ebola panic in
America was two years before all that, November 4, 2012—
the day Barack Obama was reelected.

It was no coincidence that Chris Christie talked about
Kaci Hickox while on the campaign trail in Florida. The
Republican freak-out around Ebola had less to do with

their sincere concern for public health than it did with mid-term elections—just a month away—and the 2016 presidential race, which was starting to heat up. Republicans saw Ebola as a winning issue, and goddamn if they weren't going to play it up. Even if it meant ignoring the doctors.

A couple of pieces of evidence . . .

First, the Far Right had done this before. In 2009, Glenn Beck tried to overrule the overwhelming opinion of the country's doctors, telling his listeners that flu shots might be a "deadly" plot orchestrated by the Obama administration. When Kathleen Sebelius, the Secretary of Health and Human Services, pushed back on this notion, Glenn's compatriot, my ol' friend El Rushbo, responded in his usual calm and measured manner: "Screw you, Ms. Sebelius! I am not going to take it," Rush said, "precisely because you're now telling me I must."[15]

Second, an American Ebola epidemic fit perfectly into the GOP's case against the president ahead of the 2014 midterms. Remember, 2014 was the moment that marked the rise of ISIS, that saw the Secret Service grilled over a series of security mishaps. The GOP's narrative was that Democrats were just not serious about the threats facing America—and that, in the president's case, he was even unserious about the threats facing him. Even before Ebola came to America, you could turn on the TV in Arizona and see ads claiming that the president was letting terrorists through the Mexican border. According to other commercials, Democratic senator Mark Udall was apparently getting ready to let ISIS attack Colorado.[16]

Ebola was just another chapter in this (fictional) tale of Democratic weakness. Even Ohio senator Rob Portman—no conservative fire-breather—subscribed to the idea that the midterms were really all about holding "the administration accountable for incompetence on issues like ISIS and Ebola."[17]

Perhaps this explains why, even as the threat ramped down, Republicans ramped up the rhetoric ahead of Election Day. For example, on October 24, two weeks ahead of the midterms, Nina Pham, the nurse who'd caught Ebola in Dallas—and one of two people with Ebola in the country—was declared "virus free." The number of infected people in the United States dropped by 50 percent! But it was that very same day when Christie announced his quarantine and Darrell Issa, the congressman in charge of a global-health committee, declared you'd get Ebola if you rode the bus with an infected person (which you wouldn't). He also compared the disease with the Spanish flu, which had killed more than 20 million people.[18]

And five days before Election Day—a moment when only one person in America had Ebola and he was on his way to being cured—Scott Brown, the Massachusetts transplant running for the U.S. Senate in New Hampshire, argued for stricter immigration laws. Brown said that his would-be constituents were worried about people entering the country "carrying some type of disease."[19]

Much like mating season on the Serengeti finds the male baboon beating his chest to demonstrate virility, the 2014 election season found Republicans saying ridiculous things all in the name of defending the American people.

Why didn't the media call Republicans out?

Eventually, some did. *The Washington Post* published a nifty little graphic showing that you were four times more likely to die from having your pajamas catch on fire than from Ebola. (Why couldn't Republicans have seized on that threat instead? A panic that requires everyone to sleep in the nude is a panic I can get behind.)[20]

One cable news anchor cut right to the heart of the bullshit. "There is politics in the mix," the anchor said. "With midterm elections coming, the party in charge needs to appear to be effectively leading. The party out of power needs to show that there is a lack of leadership. . . . We do not have an outbreak of Ebola in the United States," he said. "Being afraid at all is the wrong thing to do. Being petrified is ridiculous.

"My best advice," the anchor concluded: "Get a flu shot."[21]

That anchor, believe it or not, was Shepard Smith, and he delivered that message on the Fox Business Channel. (See, I give credit where credit is due even if it's due to Fox.)

Until the Republicans trounced the Democrats in the midterms, however, not enough people saw the Ebola panic for what it was—a political ploy. Suddenly, after Election Day, Republicans stopped talking about the virus! The number of cable news segments on Ebola dropped off and never bounced back.

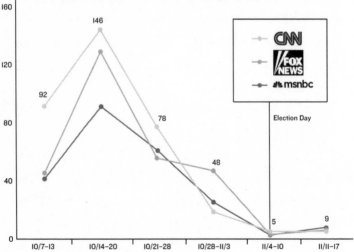

EBOLA SEGMENTS ON EVENING CABLE NEWS

Why did the coverage decrease? Well, it wasn't Ebola that changed. It was the politics.

Of all the people to opine on the politics of the Ebola

crisis, I think Kaci Hickox, the nurse locked up in the Ebola tent in Newark, said it best: "Christie [and other politicians] decided to disregard medical science and the Constitution in hopes of advancing careers. They bet that, by multiplying the existing fear and misinformation about Ebola—a disease most Americans know little about—they could ultimately manipulate everyone and proclaim themselves the protectors of the people by 'protecting' the public from a disease that hasn't killed a single American."[22]

I give her credit. If I'd been wrongly imprisoned in Chris Christie's Ebola tent for a weekend, I'd have used far more four-letter words.

In fact, let me translate Kaci's message into Carville speak.

This is bullshit.

ANTI-ANTIVAXERS

Donald J. Trump ✓
@realDonaldTrump   ✿   Following

I am being proven right about massive vaccinations—the doctors lied. Save our children & their future.

RETWEETS   LIKES
886   723

9:30 AM - 3 Sep 2014

Look at you, Donald! There's a book's worth of crazy packed inside 140 characters.

Unfortunately, Trump's position linking vaccines to issues like autism may be the most Democratic position he took during the 2016 campaign.

The Democratic Party isn't like the GOP, which runs antiscience candidates for office—Ebola doomsayers and climate change deniers. That's not us. We don't encourage antivaxers to run for dogcatcher, let alone the White House. But that doesn't mean liberal voters always immunize their kids.

The polling shows that the idiocy is roughly split on this: 34 percent of Republicans believe parents should choose whether to allow their kids to become unvaccinated deadly viral vectors while that number is about 22 percent for Democrats. But Dems are less likely to believe that vaccinating children is safe.[23]

To quote Shakespeare, there is "a pox on both our houses." Literally.

I'm an equal-opportunity criticizer. If I'm gonna take Republicans to the woodshed for fear mongering on Ebola, then I'm not going to pull punches for Democrats who think they know better than the MDs.

So here is my thinking: The science is clear on

this. There's no link between vaccines and autism—or any other childhood disorder. The only thing parents who don't vaccinate accomplish is turning their kids into potential patient zeros for eighteenth-century diseases like measles.

So I have a proposal: Let's open up the labs at the Centers for Disease Control and Prevention in Atlanta where we store samples of diseases like measles. If parents don't want to vaccinate their kids, fine. But they should have to spend ten minutes in that lab first without a biohazard suit. If that doesn't convince them, I give up.

Just let the parents know that once they're in the measles lab, we're locking the door behind them.

LESSON 2

If the Overwhelming Number of Experts Disagree with the People Telling You to Panic . . . IT'S BULLSHIT!

During the Obamacare debate, you could've taken your golf clubs to the steps of the U.S. Capitol, teed off, and chances were you'd hit at least one Republican who was foaming at

the mouth, decrying Democrats for getting between patients and their doctors. This argument struck me as the
height of hypocrisy, considering that's exactly what Republicans had done to one Florida family five years prior. All Republicans needed to do was dig through their press clippings
from 2005 and find the stories about Terri Schiavo. Then
they'd see which party comes between patients and doctors.

THIS IS A CASE STUDY IN WHAT HAPPENS WHEN YOU CON-
tradict the experts.

If you need a refresher on Terri's story, here it is: One
morning in 1990, Michael Schiavo awoke to find his wife,
Terri, collapsed and unresponsive on their hallway floor.
Why did she collapse? Doctors never determined the cause.
But the result was that oxygen stopped circulating to her
brain, leading to devastating neurological damage.

After years of therapy and treatment, Terri showed no
signs of improvement. She could roll her head and blink
her eyes, which gave her family and friends hope, but for all
intents and purposes, she was brain damaged beyond repair. Doctors diagnosed her as being in a "persistent vegetative state." There was no chance of recovery.

Terri's parents, strict Catholics and bereaved, wanted
medical officials to keep their daughter "alive" by continuing to feed and treat her. But her husband and legal guard-

ian argued that Terri, his wife, would've never wanted to live that way.

Since Terri had no will, the case went before a judge, who cited the "overwhelming credible evidence" that Terri Schiavo was "totally unresponsive"; that she had "severe structural brain damage"; and that "to a large extent her brain has been replaced by spinal fluid." He agreed that Terri's husband was allowed to remove her feeding tube and let her die.

"Done and ordered," the judge wrote.[24]

Except it wasn't.

The story of Terri Schiavo began as a local legal case and a tragic family drama, and if America was a fair and just place, it would've stayed that way. Terri would've passed on soon after the decision. Her family would have grieved. It all would've been very sad and private.

Unfortunately, Jeb Bush—who was Florida's governor, but who perhaps thought he was the Pope in Rome—tried to overrule the courts. He stirred up a national panic over Terri's right to die that included cameos from his brother, the president of the United States; the Religious Right; and, worst of all, Terri's doctors, who were effectively put on trial on the floor of the United States Congress.

By the time Washington, D.C., inserted itself into Terri's case, in 2005, Republicans—and, sadly, a few Democrats—had seen videos of Terri nodding and blinking, and started playing armchair physician. They questioned whether the doctors were right, whether Terri was in fact brain damaged beyond repair. But they had no evidence to the contrary. Every doctor who had examined Terri agreed she had no chance of recovery.

To be fair, this wasn't everyone's rationale for disagreeing with the courts. I can't fault people who sympathized with Terri's parents and their desire to keep her alive. I, too, can understand why they argued what they argued. I have daughters. (Then again, if I were in Terri's situation, I'd want someone to do what Michael Schiavo did—pull the plug. Hell, just load up my IV with brown liquor and let me go to greener pastures.)

No, the most ridiculous argument wasn't that Congress was morally right but that it was *medically right.* In front of C-SPAN cameras, spin doctors pretended to be actual doctors: "[Terri] talks and she laughs and she expresses happiness and discomfort. . . . [She's unable to speak because] she's not been afforded any speech therapy—none," said Tom DeLay, the House majority leader, who apparently believed that a couple of video clips and the votes of Texas's 22nd congressional district gave him a medical degree.[25]

Then there was Senator George Allen of Virginia, who had no medical training either: "When I observed her on videotapes," he said, "clearly [she] is conscious and has the ability to feel."[26]

Or there was Bill Frist, the Senate majority leader, who'd been a heart surgeon before he was a politician. He should've known better than to diagnose someone without examining her firsthand. But apparently his right-wing, holy-roller street cred was more important. "That footage, to me," Frist said, "depicted something very different than [a] persistent vegetative state."[27] (Thirty-one of Frist's classmates from Harvard Medical School sent him a letter saying he had used his medical degree improperly.)[28]

Washington is a town where the only thing bigger than the monuments are the egos. Still, I'm amazed by the number of politicians who believed they were qualified to give a second opinion on Terri Schiavo—and by their lack of penitence when they were proven wrong.

The political panic delayed the removal of Terri's feeding tube but ultimately could not stop it. In March 2005 Congress passed something called Terri's Law, which allowed the Schiavo case to be taken out of the Florida courts, where the judge had ordered that Michael Schiavo could remove Terri's feeding tube. Instead, there would be a new hearing in a federal court. The case went to the U.S. Court of Appeals, where, in the end, the original decision was upheld: Terri had the right to die.

And after Terri died, her autopsy established the permanence of her physical condition. She had suffered severe irreversible brain damage that left her brain discolored and scarred, shriveled to half its normal size and damaged in nearly all of its regions. She couldn't see. She couldn't feel. The brain scan showed an immense cavern of black in what should have been an area populated with healthy cells. There wasn't a neuron left.[29]

Did Republicans express regret about their misdiagnosis? No. Just as Chris Christie stood by his decision to put a healthy woman in an Ebola tent, the supporters of Terri's Law never apologized. If anything, they only denied that they'd played doctor. As Bill Frist said, "I never, never, on the floor of the Senate, made a diagnosis, nor would I ever do that."[30] (Uhhhhh, we have the tape, Senator.)

It turns out Congress does have one advantage over people with an MD. Unlike doctors, congressmen and congresswomen can't be sued for malpractice.

LESSON 3　　　**If the Panic Involves the Clintons . . . IT'S BULLSHIT!**

Let me begin with a disclaimer: I have no insider information—none, zero, zilch, nada—when it comes to the Hillary Clinton e-mail "scandal." I did not correspond with Secretary Clinton during her tenure at the State Department. I have not been to the Clinton home in Chappaqua, New York, to inspect the servers and wouldn't know what to look for if I had. Nor does the FBI brief me on their investigations, including their search into Secretary Clinton's handling of classified information.

So, no. There's no new intel here. None at all. Much to my publisher's chagrin, I do not have any new evidence to share about this whole e-mail situation, no bombshells.

Nevertheless, I feel fairly confident about the outcome of this controversy. In fact, I would wager on it . . . and wager big. I would bet whatever's in my wallet—my cash, my credit cards, my AARP membership. I'd bet it all that my opinion on this e-mail "scandal" is right, and my opinion is this:

It. Is. Bullshit.

Why am I so certain? Why would I bet the ranch when I have no more information than your average Joe Cable-News-Watcher? Well, it's not because I know the future—I don't. But I do know the past. I've had a front-row seat to every media sideshow involving the Clintons' supposed misdeeds since 1992. I've watched the Republican Party, aided and abetted by the press, jump from one Clinton controversy to the next. I've been there from Whitewater to Travelgate to Benghazi, and I've found that all of these "scandals" have one thing in common: None of them ever amounted to jack squat.

I cannot count the number of times that someone has whispered to me that whatever new Clinton "scandal" is "THE BIG ONE." Usually it's someone from the D.C. cocktail-party circuit, and they say that they "have it on good authority." They claim that "when the truth comes out, it's going to be *baaaaaaaad*." But then the truth does come out, and it never is.

The very simple reason for this is that these Clinton "scandals" aren't based on any fact or truth. They're not noble inquisitions into the character and competence of America's most distinguished female leader. These "scandals" are about one thing—politics, plain and simple.

They're about cynical, gross, and often sexist politics.

Benghazi is the perfect example. You're familiar with the story. In September of 2012, a terrorist attack—which was first reported as a spontaneous uprising—killed five Americans at the U.S. consulate in Libya. Among the dead was the American ambassador, Chris Stevens. A tragedy. And in the aftermath, Republicans accused the Obama administration, including Secretary of State Clinton, of lying about the attack and even issuing a "stand down" order to the Marines who were on their way to help. The secretary herself was accused of denying extra security to our diplomats in Libya.

All of these charges were bogus.

Between 2013 and 2015, Republicans in Congress conducted seven investigations into Benghazi, more than all of the investigations into 9/11, the USS *Cole* bombing, and the Boston Marathon attacks combined. They reviewed 70,000 documents from the State Department, spent $20 million in taxpayer dollars, and published eleven reports.[31] And they came to a conclusion: There was "no stand down order issued by or to intelligence community personnel, and there was no denial of air support to intelligence community officers on the ground."[32] Moreover, *The Washington Post* gave four Pinocchios to the claim that Secretary Clinton personally denied our diplomats more security. None of it ever happened.[33]

But this is not the end of the story. It is just the beginning. Because what does the Republican Party do when their investigation of a Democrat finds no wrongdoing? Do they hang up their jerseys? Do they put away their cleats? No, sir. No, ma'am. They most certainly do not. They don't quit investigating a Democrat, especially when that Democrat has the surname of Clinton and is the party's likely nominee for president.

When the seventh investigation into Benghazi concluded, the GOP decided to keep going. They essentially said, "Maybe the eighth time will be the charm," and they put together another committee—the Benghazi Select Committee.

I, for one, am very glad they did this because it was during the course of this eighth investigation that the GOP let slip their rationale for scrutinizing Secretary Clinton. And I can tell you what that rationale was, but you should probably hear it straight from the horse's mouth instead. Let me introduce you to Congressman Kevin McCarthy, Republican of California, who at this point in our story was the front-runner to succeed John Boehner as Speaker of the House.

Here's what McCarthy said on Fox News.

REP. McCARTHY: "Everybody thought Hillary Clinton was unbeatable. But we put together a Benghazi special committee, a select committee. What are her numbers today? Her numbers are dropping."[34]

That's right. According to McCarthy, the leader-in-waiting of the GOP, the Benghazi investigation wasn't about truth or justice or the American way. It was about Hillary Clinton's poll numbers and a strategic effort to drag them down.

When I heard this, you would've needed a crane to pick my jaw up off the floor. I was stunned. I was flabbergasted. I looked more than ever like a real-life version of Edvard Munch's *The Scream*. I've told you that when Republicans take a position they never reveal the true reason why. They lie. Well, this is the one time that the GOP let their guard slip. *They actually told the truth!* And the truth was that their investigation was political. It was designed to make Hillary lose the election.

It was bullshit.

THERE'S AN OLD SAW IN POLITICS—"HE GOT IN TROUBLE for telling the truth." For Kevin McCarthy, that certainly was the case. His comments torpedoed his bid for Speaker, the position that eventually went to the Great Conservative Hope™, Paul Ryan.

Hillary Clinton, however, has faced the opposite problem of Kevin McCarthy and most other pols. Hillary falls into trouble when other people lie about her.

For thirty years, the GOP has lied in an effort to knock Hillary out of the political arena and maybe to even put her behind bars. Of course, they've never been successful and never will be. Because there's no corruption there, no there there. I know some cynics call Republicans "fascists," but at least when the GOP puts on a show trial, they can't convict. And yet, this isn't unequivocally great news for the person on trial. In America, the taint of the accusation never fully goes away.

Yes, the GOP has failed to knock Hillary out, but that

doesn't mean they haven't damaged her reputation. It's no great secret that pollsters find Hillary's "honest and trustworthy" numbers to be lower than most politicians'. Kevin McCarthy was right about one thing—after countless investigations, Republicans have changed the way the American people see Hillary Clinton.

Which brings us back to the State Department e-mails.

If you want to hold this latest example of Republican mudslinging against Hillary Clinton, that is your prerogative, I suppose. But I prefer to look at it a different way. Hillary Clinton is the most scrutinized politician in American history. Period. She's been on the national stage for three decades during a time when the media's magnifying glass is more powerful and intrusive than ever before. You might quibble with some of the decisions she has made and how she's handled the spotlight. Republicans certainly do. But to them—and to all—I issue a challenge.

Imagine you were in her heels.

Imagine you lived the past thirty years in full view of the public.

Imagine that along the way there was a political party, supported by half the country, that tried to impeach your husband and accused you of countless crimes.

Imagine eight different congressional committees that investigated you with the announced intent to drive your favorability ratings down.

Could you honestly say that you'd escape that kind of scrutiny without a scratch?

I can tell you one thing. If someone spent all that energy investigating me, I'd be serving five to ten for a truly shocking amount of jaywalking and public urination.

THE CLINTON SEX SCANDAL, TWENTY YEARS LATER

The legendary Chinese general Sun Tzu had a proverb. "If you wait by the river long enough," he said, "the bodies of your enemies will float by."

I've gotta give General Sun some credit. He lived in China two thousand years ago, but he absolutely nailed what it's been like living on the shores of the Potomac River in the twenty years since the Monica Lewinsky scandal.

You might remember that back in the '90s, the Republican Party used a sex scandal to try to accomplish what they twice couldn't do in an election: keep President Clinton out of the White House. There were many vicious, vitriolic, petty critics who made it their mission to savage the president in the press and in Congress.

Well, in the twenty years since, I've been keeping

tabs on those critics, and what do you know, it's been uncovered that a lot of those individuals committed the same devious deeds they criticized the president for. And some did far, far worse.

For twenty years, I've been waiting by the river, and one by one, the enemies have floated on by.

There was Newt Gingrich of course, the former Speaker of the House. His bloated gasbag of a body bounced up and down on the Potomac waters after it was revealed that he was cheating on his wife while calling for Clinton's impeachment. His excuse for the affair was that he "was driven by how passionately [he] felt about this country." (I tell ya right now, there's only one way that excuse is true, and it's if Newt named his manhood "this country." To be fair, Newt is the type of guy who would do that.)[35]

Floating down the river right next to Newt were Congressmen Henry Hyde (R-IL) and Bob Livingston (R-LA). Both called for Clinton's impeachment, even though both had carried on affairs of their own. Bob Livingston had been involved with four women and resigned on the day of the impeachment vote. Henry Hyde, however, hung on to his congressional seat. He attributed his affair to "youthful indiscretion," even though he was forty years old at the time he bumped uglies with someone who was not his wife. (Maybe that's why the GOP has a problem with the youth vote? You're a "youth" until you have regularly scheduled colonoscopies.)[36]

Nor should we forget about ol' Dennis Hastert, the guy who took the Speaker of the House job when Newt Gingrich resigned. In 1998 Hastert said his "conscience" demanded that he impeach Bill Clinton, which in retrospect may be the most hypocritical thing said in the history of mankind. You see, Hastert was recently sentenced to fifteen months in prison for paying hush money to a former student he'd sexually abused. (Hastert had been a high school wrestling coach back in the 1960s and '70s). The judge presiding over Hastert's trial called him a "serial child molester." I'd also call him "one of the more despicable hypocrites to ever walk the Earth."[37]

The final body floating down the Potomac on its way to the deep waters of the Atlantic? That belongs to Kenneth Starr, the independent prosecutor who investigated President Clinton's sex life with the self-piety of an old church lady and the viciousness of a junkyard dog hopped up on cocaine. I hadn't heard much about Ken Starr's recent life until right before the deadline for this book. News broke that Starr had been ousted from his new job as the head of Baylor University. Why? Because he'd been looking the other way while members of Baylor's football team were reported for sexual assault.

Twenty years after Starr twisted Monica Lewinsky's arm, trying to get her to speak up about having sex with Bill Clinton, Starr's university has been accused of failing to speak up for rape victims. (Just let the infuriating hypocrisy of that contradiction wash over you.)[38]

As a Catholic, I very rarely tell people to "go to hell." But for Gingrich, Hyde, Livingston, Hastert, and Starr, I'm willing to make an exception. According to Dante, there are nine circles in Hell, and the eighth—or second-hottest—is reserved for the hypocrites. Well, I hope Dante is right—and that the devil turns up the thermostat when our five friends arrive.

THE BOYS WHO CRIED EBOLA! . . . AND BENGHAZI! . . . AND NOT BRAIN-DEAD!

Let's wrap up this lecture on bullshit with a story. It's the tale of the "Boy Who Cried Wolf."

I don't remember when I first heard about "The Boy Who Cried Wolf," but I was probably very young and very underwhelmed. As a kid, I was never afraid of wolves. Louisiana doesn't really have wolves. For us, a more accurate title might've been "The Boy Who Cried Alligator."

Nevertheless, I picked up on the gist of the story pretty quickly. The message was simple even for a hick like me: Don't keep telling people to panic when they shouldn't. Because they will stop listening to you. And you will die. (There's nothing like a bedtime story that ends with a small child being eaten alive!)

My kids are in college now, so I have no idea if parents still tell this story to their children, but my guess is that if they do, the lesson doesn't pack the same punch. Hell, the moral of the story isn't even true anymore. You *can* keep crying wolf! There's an entire political party that proves it. You can cry wolf—or Ebola! or Benghazi! or Terri's Not Brain-Dead!—and the whole goddamn country keeps listening.

Today the boy who cried wolf isn't eaten alive. He's running for president.

Indeed, crying wolf is now a viable political strategy and one with very few repercussions. You can shout something crazy and wrong, and when that panic flames out, you can just move on to the next one. You don't even have to acknowledge your past mistakes. Here are a couple of head-lines you'll never read:

CONGRESS: WHOOPS! TERRI SCHIAVO BRAIN-DEAD
AFTER ALL. OUR BAD.

GOP TO HILLARY: YOU GOT US! WE WERE TOTALLY JUST
TRYING TO SCREW YOU WITH BENGHAZI.

The feedback loop that rewards leaders who speak the truth and punishes ones who spout bullshit is broken. I wish I could fix it, but unfortunately, no one is handing me the keys to Fox News headquarters. So the best I can do is conclude this lecture with a couple of tips.

LISTEN TO THE EXPERTS. This might sound like a novel con-cept, but the people who *study* issues for a living know bet-ter than the people who *yell* about issues for a living. If the person talking is wearing a lab coat, listen to them. If they're wearing an American flag pin and rolling up their shirtsleeves just because it makes them look relatable, cover your ears.

FOLLOW THE THREE DAY RULE. During my younger years, there was something called the Three Date Rule, which said that if you make it to the end of date number three, the date would likely last until the following morning . . . if you catch my drift.

I can't personally vouch for this rule. It never seemed to work for me. But, fortunately, I have a corollary. It's designed to *prevent* you from getting screwed . . . by the media, in particular. It's called the Three Day Rule.

April Fools' Day, it's been said, is the only day in America when we skeptically evaluate news stories before accepting them as true. There's something wrong with that. It's wise to wait and research before forming an opinion. I withhold judgment for about three days on any story after it breaks. After all, the whole story never comes out on the first day, and most things are usually more complicated than can be conveyed in a headline crawl across the bottom of your TV screen.

WATCH FOX FOR FUN, NOT FACTS. I say this as a former Fox News contributor. There's no doubt that Fox is successful at what it does, but what it does is "news entertainment"— not news. Today it's good business to mix news, opinion, and showmanship, and Fox is the best at doing all three. So, by all means, continue watching O'Reilly and Hannity and the gang. It's always good to know what the other side is thinking. But whatever you do, don't believe them.

Where We Were Wrong

When I wrote the first version of this book, in 1996, I filled it with some BOLD IDEAS for how readers could get involved in politics. One of my fantastic recommendations was the following: "Get involved in discussions on the Internet," I wrote, "Although I personally have a better chance of flying a 747 than I do of finding the on-off switch on my office computer, I hear the Internet is a great way to get involved and stay informed."

Hoo boy! When I read that again after twenty years, I wanted to hide my head under a very large blanket out of embarrassment. Is there any statement more dated than "I hear the Internet is a great way to get involved"? I do not think so.

I was even more embarrassed to see that I also provided a "quick list of ways you can find good Dems in cyberspace." This included visiting the White House's website and subscribing to something called "the Demtalk list server." "[S]end the message 'subscribe' (no quotes) to Demtalk-list@aquilapub.clever.net," I advised. (If you e-mail that address today, it'll bounce back with the message "permanently failed.")

Why do I mention any of this? Well, because my opinion about the Internet isn't the only one that's failed to hold up.

If I'm going to talk about flaws in the Republican Party, you better believe that I'm going to devote some ink to where Democrats have fouled up. And before I have this book bound and shipped, one issue where we need to set the record straight is on energy.

An article from *The New York Times*'s Eduardo Porter recently caught my attention. It was titled "Liberal Biases, Too, May Block Progress on Climate Change."

Porter's argument was clear: It's well-known that, right now, nuclear power is the only technology that can generate a lot of energy at a price comparable to greenhouse-gas-emitting power sources. This is why the majority of scientists favor more nuclear power as a way to combat climate change. And yet polls show that only a minority of Democrats—35 percent—favor building additional nuclear plants. Republicans, on the other hand, support nuclear to the tune of 60 percent.

"[On nuclear, it] is the G.O.P [that's] closer to the scientific consensus," Porter wrote.[1]

Usually, those would be fightin' words for any good liberal, me included, but I don't disagree with Porter. In fact, I think he's right. Republicans may be against the science behind global warming, but when it comes to solving the problem, Democrats need a lesson from someone in a lab coat.

Of course, I am not the right person to teach that lesson. I'm no scientist. Hell, I graduated LSU with a 4.0 . . . blood alcohol level. So to help disabuse Democrats of our illusions, I called up a real scientist. I spoke with our friend Richard Muller of the Berkeley Earth Science Temperature Project and heard his thoughts on stopping global warming.

What follows is our conversation, which I've edited for easier reading.

JAMES CARVILLE: So, Dr. Muller, your theory is that the climate is getting warmer, that carbon is contributing to the warming, and that there are some practical steps that we can take to alleviate the problem?

RICHARD MULLER: Yes. That's right. I have what I call the triad. There are three steps that I think we can take, which I hope would forge an alliance between Republicans and Democrats and independents.

The first step is an improved program of energy conservation, because energy conservation is free energy. It's a huge step.

JAMES CARVILLE: Like Jimmy Carter telling us to all wear sweaters?

RICHARD MULLER: Actually, I think Jimmy Carter did a bit of a disservice to the conservation movement. It shouldn't be about turning down the thermostat and taking cold showers because telling people they have to suffer isn't a very effective strategy. We should be focusing on things like home insulation, more efficient machines and appliances.

JAMES CARVILLE: Fair point. What's the second step?

RICHARD MULLER: Natural gas. I see natural gas as a very important bridge fuel for the next thirty or forty years, maybe longer, in order to reduce global warming.

The key thing here is China. Because whatever we do in the United States is inconsequential unless it has an impact on the way energy is produced in China and the developing world. China is undergoing enormous growth. They're now producing twice the CO_2 we are every year, and a lot of that comes from coal. If China could develop natural gas instead of developing coal, then we could make a meaningful dent in carbon emissions. Natural gas has about one-half to one-third of the effect on carbon emissions as coal does.

JAMES CARVILLE: This is the kind of question a scientist hates, but I have to ask it anyway. What about renewables—solar and wind, for example? What do you think is the time, a logical time frame for when the renewables will kick in?

RICHARD MULLER: I think right now renewables can be afforded by the developed world. But if you look at the numbers, the fraction of energy in China that comes from renewables is 0.0006. It's minuscule.

JAMES CARVILLE: I'm not a scientist, but that's a small number.

RICHARD MULLER: Yeah. It's a small number. It is well less than 1 percent of China's energy. The problem is they're too expensive for the developing world. That's why I favor natural gas as a bridge fuel. We need that time to get renewables cheap enough that the developing world can afford them.

JAMES CARVILLE: And what's your third step?

RICHARD MULLER: The last one is nuclear. I have a team that does scientific consulting for different organizations and even some countries. And based on our research, we now are favoring the major expansion of nuclear power.

There are many objections with nuclear, but we have looked at them all, and we believe that nuclear is competitive with coal, and safer, much, much safer than coal, far more practical than current-day renewables.

That's the triad. The triad is energy conservation, natural gas, and nuclear.

JAMES CARVILLE: Well, Dr. Muller, I appreciate your time, and I have to say I think you've done a really admirable thing. You were a guy who had a question about global warming, and you went out there and tested it yourself. You actually took it upon yourself to find the truth. That doesn't happen very often, I've just got to say, certainly not in the political world.

RICHARD MULLER: I'm pleased that you say that. If I'm playing such a role, then I'm very proud of having done that. I think part of the greatest loss that has taken place in this field has been a loss of confidence in science. Part of that has come about because of people exaggerating. No matter which side they're on, they're exaggerating. We hope we've established a reputation for being objective, and we would like to leverage that by continuing to be objective when talking about ways to slow and stop global warming.

Trump's Original Sin

Unless you've been living under a rock—or in front of a television that only airs Fox News—you know that African Americans in this country still face some soul-crushing discrimination and injustice. I certainly don't want to speak for anyone on this subject. I think there are a lot of people telling important truths right now, including the Black Lives Matter movement, and I wouldn't presume to lecture on their behalf.

But when it comes to race and politics, I do feel obligated to point out something that the media didn't point out enough during the primaries: that the Republican Party has taken a hard turn for the worse on issues of race.

In the twenty years prior to Trump, the GOP's strategy for handling the widespread legacy of racism had been to silence any talk of it. Look at the killing of Trayvon Martin, for example. When President Obama weighed in on that tragedy—*"If I had a son, he'd look like Trayvon"*—the airwaves were screeching with conservatives saying that the president should butt out, that it was a local issue. (If I recall correctly, "it's a local issue" was also the argument that the Confederacy made to Mr. Lincoln about slavery; but no matter.)

This hands-off approach to racism was offensive and wrong, but it isn't nearly as bad as Trump's. After all, Trump doesn't merely tiptoe around the issue of race. Instead, he uses his shiny black leather Oxfords to kick dirt in the face of any individual who doesn't share his ethnicity or skin color. (Well, no one really shares Trump's skin color. But you get my point.)

Let me be real clear about this: When it comes to race, Donald Trump appeals to the worst in people. His approach to race relations is disgusting. Trump's policies—e.g., the ban on Muslims—are discriminatory, to say the least. You could also look at his life before politics, which is shameful too. In 1989 Trump took out full-page ads in newspapers calling on New York to bring back the death penalty; he wanted to execute five black and Hispanic fourteen-year-olds who'd been accused and convicted of raping a jogger in Central Park. Well, it turns out that the Central Park Five were later exonerated for that crime when the real criminal was caught and his DNA matched the evidence.

(Trump still believes the boys were guilty. "They did not exactly have the pasts of angels," he's said.)[1]

No doubt about it. All of this is horrible. But what concerns me most about Trump's bigotry is that it's now a central part of his political strategy. He uses racism like a cudgel, as a way to gain power.

The press, in my opinion, has largely overlooked this, and there's no better example than the act that launched Trump's career in Republican politics: birtherism.

I'M A CATHOLIC, AND I'VE SEEN ENOUGH BAPTISMAL WATER spilled to fill William Taft's bathtub ten times over. But it doesn't take a Catholic like me to understand the original sin of the Donald Trump candidacy. His first act on the political stage was to declare himself the head of the birther movement. For Trump, the year 2011 began with the BIG NEWS that he had rejected Lindsay Lohan for *Celebrity Apprentice*, but by April, his one-man show to paint Barack Obama as a secret Kenyan had become the talk of the country. Five years later, Trump has likely locked up the Republican nomination for president.[2]

In many ways, birtherism is what launched Trump's campaign. And as I write this, Trump has still refused to disavow his preposterous conspiracy theory. The last time Trump addressed the question was in July 2015, when

Anderson Cooper pressed him on whether President Obama was, in fact, born in the United States. Trump's response was, "I really don't know." Since then, Trump has remained silent—and largely unchallenged—on the issue.[3]

I'm taxing my mind to find a historical comparison here, to put this in context. I suppose Trump's birtherism is the intellectual equivalent of the flat-earth theory; both are fully contradicted by the evidence. But then again, there is a difference between the two, and the difference is this: If a presidential candidate insisted that the USS *Theodore Roosevelt* would fall off the edge of the map after sailing past Catalina Island, Wolf Blitzer would probably ask him about it. That hasn't happened with Trump.

There were twelve debates during the Republican primaries, six televised forums, and enough cable interviews to combust a DVR, but the only "birther" issue extensively covered in the press was whether Senator Ted Cruz was ineligible to be president because he was born in Calgary Flames territory.

It's now known among reporters that Obama's birthplace is a strictly verboten topic for Trump. If you bring up the subject, as Chris Matthews did in December, Trump looks at you with a glare I assume he otherwise reserves for undocumented immigrants and says, "I don't talk about that anymore." Most reporters seem unwilling to piss off The Donald and risk losing their access.[4]

Look, I understand that there's plenty of craziness to investigate with Trump. The man spouts more nutty theories and stomach-turning offensiveness than a YouTube comments section. But his birtherism deserves extra scrutiny. It's more toxic than, say, Trump's belief that vaccines cause autism. Because it's possible to be an anti-vaxxer and not be a bigot, but it's impossible to be a birther and not be one.

Birtherism is "a conscious form of race-baiting," to use a phrase from David Remnick, the editor of *The New Yorker* magazine.[5] It's no different from what the militantly segregationist Alabama governor George Wallace did back in the sixties or what Ronald Reagan did when he campaigned in the South and railed against "strapping young bucks" using food stamps to buy steak.[6] This is rhetoric that divides the country along racial lines. It's a segregating form of politics. And the scariest thing about Trump is that it's a core part of his political philosophy.

By his own admission, Trump sees the controversy over Obama's birthplace as foundational to his brand and instructive of how he approaches politics. In 2013, when ABC asked him about his aggressive birtherism, he said, "I don't think I went overboard. Actually, I think it made me very popular . . . I do think I know what I'm doing."[7]

Let that statement sink in for a second: When it comes to birtherism, Trump believes "it made [him] very popular" and that he "knows what he's doing." I've been working with candidates for half a century, and I can tell you that after a statement like that, it should've surprised no one that Trump followed his foray into the birther movement with a parade of even more racism. When politicians find a strategy that works, they just keep repeating it. Which is what Trump did. He followed up his birtherism by calling Mexicans "rapists," then proposing to ban Muslims, and then failing to denounce the Ku Klux Klan.

Indeed, with birtherism, Trump discovered a sad truth about modern American politics: Bigotry gets you attention. And as long as you bring viewers, readers, and clicks, the fourth estate will let you get away with that bigotry.

No doubt about it. At least on race, Donald Trump knows what he's doing.

LONG BEFORE DONALD TRUMP, THERE WAS ANOTHER demagogue, Huey Long, who also made a run for the White House. Long was fictionalized and immortalized as the character Willie Stark in Robert Penn Warren's novel *All the King's Men*, in which Warren wrote, "Man is conceived in sin and born in corruption."

So, too, was Trump's political career.

The media should never overlook that—and nor should the country.

TRUMP STEAK™ WITH SIZZLING VEGETABLES

If you happen to have your hands on a Trump Steak™, congratulations! You have a very well-aged cut of beef.

That's because Trump Steaks™ sold so poorly that The Donald stopped selling them years ago. The steak in your possession probably spent a decade sitting in the Sharper Image stockroom.

Even I can't salvage a sirloin like that, but I can tell you how to prepare perfect vegetables to mask the taste.

INGREDIENTS

- 1 head of garlic, minced
- 2 red onions, peeled and sliced horizontally
- 2 stalks of broccoli, chopped

DIRECTIONS

Place vegetables in tinfoil, generously sprinkle them with salt and pepper, and then drizzle them with olive oil. Wrap up the vegetables and place them directly on top of the grill. Let sit for 10 to 15 minutes. Remove and carefully slit open the tin foil.

I'd Sooner Work for Kim Jong-un

You've probably noticed that something has been missing in this book—I haven't talked much about foreign affairs yet. So far, I've stayed strictly inside the borders of the USA, which, the GOP willing, will soon be a crime if you are a foreign-born Muslim.

I certainly could talk at length about America's place in the world and how Republicans managed to screw that up (ahem, Iraq), but that's well-tilled soil by now. Besides, if the Republican Party is going to occupy the State Department anytime soon, it'll be under a very different kind of commander in chief. It's Donald Trump's party now, and this is a man who consults only himself when it comes to matters of international import. In fact, he's bragged about it: "I'm speaking with myself, number one," he's said, "because I have a very good brain."[1]

Well, I thought I'd put that statement to the test: Does Trump really have a very good brain when it comes to foreign affairs? And to free our discussion of liberal bias, I won't do any talking. Instead, I'll leave the opinion on Trump's mind up to some of his fellow Republicans, all of whom have spent a lifetime honing their expertise on international issues. Here's a sampler of what Republicans have said about Donald Trump and foreign affairs:

"I would sooner work for Kim Jong-un than for Donald Trump. I think Donald Trump is objectively more dangerous than Kim Jong-un and not as stable."

—MAX BOOT, SENIOR FELLOW AT THE COUNCIL ON FOREIGN RELATIONS AND FORMER FOREIGN-POLICY ADVISOR TO MITT ROMNEY[2]

"Donald Trump . . . I view his current statements as erratic . . . I just don't know what it is he's going to do. [On the other hand,] I have seen some performance on the part of Secretary Clinton . . . This is an experienced diplomat. This is an experienced woman who seems to have taken these questions seriously."

—GENERAL MICHAEL HAYDEN, CIA DIRECTOR UNDER GEORGE W. BUSH, RESPONDING TO THE QUESTION: WHO IS A LARGER THREAT TO THE MAINTENANCE OF AMERICA'S FOREIGN POLICY, DONALD TRUMP OR HILLARY CLINTON?[3]

"We've got a lot of problems today, but you'd have a
hell of a lot more if that were the case."

—JAMES BAKER, SECRETARY OF STATE FOR GEORGE H. W. BUSH
AND SECRETARY OF THE TREASURY AND CHIEF OF STAFF FOR
RONALD REAGAN, RESPONDING TO TRUMP'S PROPOSALS
TO PULL OUT OF NATO OR ALLOW SOUTH KOREA AND
JAPAN TO OBTAIN NUCLEAR WEAPONS[4]

"Trump's toxic brew of protectionism and isolationism is
straight from the history books, unfortunately from the
chapters when frightened democracies tried to retreat, only to
worsen their own economic recession and give evil
aggressors room to accomplish their aims."

—JENNIFER RUBIN, CONSERVATIVE WRITER FOR
THE WASHINGTON POST[5]

"Are we sure the guy running the teleprompter has the pages
in the right order . . . Trump's speech was pathetic in terms of
understanding the role America plays in the world . . .
Ronald Reagan must be rolling over in his grave."

—SENATOR LINDSEY GRAHAM, TWEETING HIS REVIEW OF DONALD
TRUMP'S FIRST MAJOR FOREIGN POLICY SPEECH[6]

"The nuclear codes should not be handed
to an erratic individual."

—SENATOR MARCO RUBIO, WHO DELIVERED THIS STATEMENT
DURING HIS CAMPAIGN AGAINST TRUMP BUT STILL STOOD
BY HIS WORDS EVEN AFTER AGREEING TO "SUPPORT"
THE PRESUMPTIVE REPUBLICAN NOMINEE[7]

And then, of course, there's this whopper of an open letter signed by more than one hundred conservative foreign policy experts:

> *[Trump's] vision of American influence and power in the world is wildly inconsistent and unmoored in principle. He swings from isolationism to military adventurism within the space of one sentence.*
>
> *His advocacy for aggressively waging trade wars is a recipe for economic disaster in a globally connected world.*
>
> *His embrace of the expansive use of torture is inexcusable.*
>
> *His hateful, anti-Muslim rhetoric undercuts the seriousness of combating Islamic radicalism by alienating partners in the Islamic world making significant contributions to the effort. Furthermore, it endangers the safety and Constitutionally guaranteed freedoms of American Muslims.*
>
> *Controlling our border and preventing illegal immigration is a serious issue, but his insistence that Mexico will fund a wall on the southern border inflames unhelpful passions, and rests on an utter misreading of, and contempt for, our southern neighbor.*
>
> *Similarly, his insistence that close allies such as Japan must pay vast sums for protection is the senti-*

ment of a racketeer, not the leader of the alliances that have served us so well since World War II.

His admiration for foreign dictators such as Vladimir Putin is unacceptable for the leader of the world's greatest democracy.

He is fundamentally dishonest. Evidence of this includes his attempts to deny positions he has un-questionably taken in the past, including on the 2003 Iraq war and the 2011 Libyan conflict. We accept that views evolve over time, but this is simply misrepresentation.

His equation of business acumen with foreign policy experience is false. Not all lethal conflicts can be resolved as a real estate deal might, and there is no recourse to bankruptcy court in international affairs.

—An open letter signed by foreign-policy experts including former Secretary of Homeland Security Michael Chertoff, former Homeland Security Advisor Frances Townsend, and former Deputy Secretary of State Robert Zoellick—all of whom served under George W. Bush[8]

Do Facts Matter Anymore?

The late New York senator Daniel Patrick Moynihan had a saying. "Everybody is entitled to his own opinion," Moynihan said, "but not his own facts."

Well, we're about at the end of this book, and by now, you've plowed through an almanac's worth of facts. I made sure this book was stuffed to the margins with them, everything from the GDP growth rate under Democratic presidents since 1952, to the cost-benefit ratio of the Clean Air Act, to the contents of Chris Christie's Ebola tent. All, I think, point to the conclusion that Democrats do a better job at governing the United States, but I can understand if you're still shrugging your shoulders. You could be forgiven for reading all those facts and asking, "So what?"

Will those facts really change anyone's mind?

Do facts even matter?

That's certainly the fashionable thing to do right now, to suggest that facts don't make a difference anymore, and if you're looking at the Republican Party, it's a hard assertion to deny. Republican voters have chosen a presidential nominee who can't go five minutes without lying, and that's not a made-up number. Journalists have actually subjected themselves to listening to hours and hours of Trump's stump speeches, and they've analyzed how often he lies. Trump's tolerance for truth is five minutes.[1]

Of course, Trump isn't the first member of the GOP to traffic in falsehoods. He may be a purveyor of more vicious untruths compared with other Republicans—like the conspiracy theory that Ted Cruz's father helped assassinate JFK or the notion that vaccines cause autism—but Trump is really just following in a long tradition of liars, cheats, and scoundrels. Long before The Donald, Republicans were claiming that food stamps were actually a detriment to hungry children and that pollution would go away if we let the market take care of it. All the Republican Party is doing now is trading those lies in for bigger, brasher ones. Lies that are worthy of giant fake-gold letters like the ones that adorn Trump Tower.

More and more, it seems we do exist in two countries. There's one that's based in reality, where tax cuts for the rich do not magically help poor people; a country where subsidized health care doesn't kill people or wreck the economy; a country that exists on Earth, a planet that is four billion years old and getting warmer. That's one America.

But there's also a second America, the country where Trump supporters, right-wingers, and conspiracy theorists live. And in this country, reality is a loose concept. In this second America, armies of Mexican rapists are coming across the border, Obamacare is about to spark the next Great Depression, and Hillary Clinton's deleted e-mails contain the real truth about Benghazi and other Illuminati secrets. This paranoid version of America is also a place where, six feet beneath the ground, Senator Moynihan is rolling in his grave.

Because now people do feel entitled to their own facts.

This is the central tension of writing about politics in 2016. If facts don't appear to matter—if logic and reason and data don't matter—then why write or read about them at all?

Well, I didn't have a good answer to that question until I spoke to a very smart man. You've met him before: Richard Muller.

I began this book with half of Muller's story, and it's only fitting that we end with the other half. After all, if there's one person who has the right to think that facts don't matter anymore, it's Muller. He has 1.6 billion data points that proved climate change is man-made, and still people think global warming is a hoax because of snowballs. If I were him, I'd be tempted to hang up my lab coat and call it quits. But when I spoke to Muller, he gave me a different perspective.

Muller told me a story.

He told me about the time he presented his data to an influential billionaire skeptic. This billionaire, I presume, was a guy like one of the Koch brothers—a hardened conservative with a stake in maintaining the fiction that the jury was out on global warming.

Muller traveled to this gentleman's office. He presented the data that he'd spent years compiling in Berkeley. He brought out his charts and his graphs, which showed rising global temperatures correlating perfectly with the increase in carbon emissions. And yet, when Muller finished his presentation, the billionaire's response was not "Wow! I'm converted," or "This data is really interesting. My mind is changed." Instead, the billionaire responded with something else.

"Well, Dr. Muller," the billionaire said, "maybe global warming will be good for us."

Maybe global warming will be good for us!?

Let me tell you something. If I'd been in that room, I would've jumped out of my chair and made that billionaire eat my presentation for saying something so jaw-droppingly stupid. But Richard Muller had a different response, which is just one of the many reasons he's a smarter man than I am. Muller didn't scream at this billionaire. He didn't jump out of his chair or pull his hair out. His face did not go purple with rage. Here is what Richard Muller did instead: he smiled.

That's right. When the billionaire pondered if global warming might be a good thing, Muller grinned from ear to ear. "I consider that a victory," Muller said, because according to him, at this point the billionaire was no longer denying that global warming was real or that it's caused by humans. Indeed, by saying that global warming might be a good thing, the billionaire had admitted that global warming exists!

"That," Muller said, "was converting an influential skeptic."[2]

Muller's story is the reason why I wrote a book like this. Facts can't convert people out of their stupid beliefs, but they can wear those beliefs down.

FOR THE PAST TWENTY YEARS, THE FACTS HAVE WORN DOWN the case for the Republican Party. This has been a book about the GOP's abysmal record over the past two decades and the Democratic Party's remarkable one. Progressives have been on the right side of history on everything from the economy, to race relations, to health care. In other words, if you've had a wallet, a conscience, or a pulse, we've been the party for you. And while Republicans would never admit that we're right and they're wrong, their arguments are starting to show it.

It's not just Muller's billionaire and global warming. Think about income inequality, for example. Today the Republican Party is led by a guy who thinks income inequality will be fixed by kicking out Mexicans and declaring trade war on China, but twenty years ago, most Republicans didn't even believe income inequality was a problem. By those standards, an America with Trump's Republican Party is a little less wrong.

Or look at gay rights. Today the conservative argument against gay rights boils down to religious freedom. A baker, for instance, shouldn't have to sell a gay couple a wedding cake because that would infringe on his Christian duty to discriminate against homosexuals. That's the Republican position, at least, and I'll give them credit for getting creative with their bigotry. But the religious freedom argument is a sad hill to die on compared with what Republicans were saying about gays just ten years ago. Back then, they argued that gay marriage was a threat to American families everywhere. Gay couples, if they were allowed to marry, were going to infiltrate your homes with their assless chaps and Madonna CDs and corrupt your kids. Think of the children, the GOP was basically saying. And next to that vitriol, talking about the rights of a homophobic baker sounds less like a rallying cry and more like a death groan of the GOP's intolerance.

This is just the beginning. Like the tidewaters that lap away at the Louisiana coastline, the rightness of Democratic policy is eroding Republican arguments. Slowly—very slowly—our logic is starting to matter. That's why Democrats can't be quiet about our record of achievement. That's why we can't be silent about the facts. Because facts take a long time to work, and we have a lot of work to do—and not much time left to do it.

We have an election in November.

Before then, we have to fight back against the idea that the poor are better off when food stamps are cut so that the richest can keep their wallets fat.

We have to dispel the fiction that all regulations are job-killers and that the market can, by itself, solve everything from smog to reckless investing.

We have to prove that America is a country where racism in politics is no longer tolerated and that anyone who practices it is unfit to lead.

And we also have to keep convincing the American public that a widening income gap is a serious threat to the American experiment.

You are now armed with the facts necessary to prove all of those points. You have, in your hands, the facts that matter. And my fondest wish is that they matter most on

November 8, 2016. That is America's day of reckoning. It's the day that'll decide whether the Democratic Party lives or dies; whether the Republican Party seizes control of the entire government or flames out and is buried in the political party graveyard next to the Whigs and the Know-Nothings and the Dixiecrats.

November 8 is Election Day.

It's the day we can finally tell the country, "We're still right, and they're still wrong."

WHERE WILL I BE ON ELECTION NIGHT THIS NOVEMBER?

Well, I'll probably be home in New Orleans, watching the returns on one TV while Mary watches them on another. We keep our home what you might call Carville Kosher on Election Day, one room for Republicans and a separate one for Democrats; one group ready to pop champagne while the other is ready to drown their sorrows with a bottle of Jack Daniel's.

That's where I'll be on Election Night—in my politically divided home. Although if I were a younger man—and a bolder one—I'd likely be somewhere else.

In fact, let me tell you where I'd be on Election Night 2016 if I had my druthers. Let me tell you about the secret wish I've been harboring since Donald Trump locked up the GOP nomination and pissed in the punch bowl of the Republican Party.

Here is my wish: On Election Night, I'd like to be in Manhattan, at 725 Fifth Avenue, otherwise known as Trump Tower. I'd like to strut through the revolving doors into the gold-plated lobby, and ascend up that escalator where Trump first declared his candidacy. I would do my damnedest to pass the Secret Service—some might remember me from the Bill Clinton days—and I'd take the elevator up to the twenty-fifth floor, where Trump keeps his office.

I don't know for sure if Trump will be in his office that night, watching the returns, but I hope he is. I hope he's there, and right as I walk through the door, the news networks call Ohio and Florida and Pennsylvania for the Democrats. I hope I'm there to see the light go out of Trump's eyes, to witness the moment that the dream of his giant orange face on Mount Rushmore dies.

I want to be there—just a fly on the wall—to watch Trump prepare his concession speech. I want to see him get ready to leave, only to realize that his throat is too dry to deliver the remarks. And I want to watch him turn around, looking for something to quench his thirst, only to see the punch bowl that his staff had prepared in case of his victory. And then I want to watch him take a looooooong sip.

Because I firmly believe that on the night of November 8, Hillary Clinton and the Democratic Party are going to return the favor to Donald Trump. I think we're going to piss in his punch bowl. And I want to be there, in person, to watch him drink it.

I want to see how Donald likes the taste.

A Voter Guide for 2016

Election law is a funny thing in America—particularly when it comes to the church parking lot. In exchange for their tax exemption, churches are legally prohibited from endorsing candidates. But the Religious Right is very good at finding loopholes, and they realized that while they cannot tell their congregation who to vote for, they can inform their churchgoers where the candidates stand on the issues.

That's why, the Sunday before Election Day, churches often paper the cars in their parking lots with "voter guides." These flyers contain valuable information for holy rollers, like which candidate supports sodomy, or killing babies, or who believes marriage should be between Adam and Steve, not Adam and Eve.

Well, in a bit of payback, I've provided my own 2016 voter guide here for y'all. This way, you can see where Trump and Hillary stand on the issues that matter.

	HILLARY CLINTON	DONALD TRUMP
GLOBAL WARMING	Is real and caused by man	Is a Chinese hoax
GUN CONTROL	Strong background checks	Sh*t happens
FEDERAL MINIMUM WAGE	Raise it	Repeal it
VACCINATIONS	One of the great scientific achievements of all time	Causes autism
HANDS	Steady	Fun-sized
MINORITY GROUPS SLANDERED	0	How many are there?
AFRICAN AMERICANS	Face systematic injustice and a legacy of racism	"Laziness is a trait in Blacks." *(Trump actually said this!)*[1]
MEXICANS	Citizens of America's third-largest trading partner and ally	Criminals, rapists, and some, I assume, are good people
MUSLIMS	Members of the world's second-largest religion	It won't be the second largest after I bomb the sh*t outta them
PERSONAL ROLE MODEL	Eleanor Roosevelt	Vladimir Putin . . . or Billy Zane's character from *Titanic* . . . either one

	HILLARY CLINTON	DONALD TRUMP
IS IT APPROPRIATE TO IMPERSONATE SOMEONE WHILE SPEAKING TO THE MEDIA?	No	Let me introduce you to my imaginary publicist, John Miller
KU KLUX KLAN	Disavowed	Um, never heard of them
POWs	Heroes	Prefers soldiers who weren't captured
MENSTRUAL CYCLES	A natural bodily function of post-pubescent females	The reason Megyn Kelly hates me
PREFERRED TERM FOR WOMAN	Woman	"Fine piece of ass"
THE WOMAN I FIND MOST BEAUTIFUL	My daughter	My daughter

ACKNOWLEDGMENTS

My experience with trying to thank everyone for coming to your party is that you usually forget to mention the governor.

Many friends—more than I can possibly name—contributed to the planning, writing, and publishing of this book. And to try to recognize everyone would inevitably mean that I forget someone. So to everyone, I'll just say, "Y'all know who you are—and thank you."

I'd be remiss, though, if I didn't recognize the hard work of a few individuals, without whom this book would still be some random Trump jokes kicking around in my skull.

David Rosenthal, my publisher, deserves all the credit for shepherding this book to the shelf and for the inspired thought that put Donald Trump's head up an elephant's rear end on the cover.

Then there's Ben Hunt, who's a Republican campaign's worst nightmare. The man has a knack for finding the most outrageous statements ever uttered by Republicans, and I appreciate his research.

And finally, I am grateful to Ryan Jacobs, who's a fine writer and idea man—and who's been as good a partner as one could hope for in writing this book.

NOTES

A Letter from the Author

1. https://www.nationalreview.com/nrd/articles/432569/father-f-hrer.

Prologue: 1.6 Billion Facts & a Snowball

1. Conversation with Richard Muller, April 26, 2011, via phone.
2. Ibid.
3. http://www.businessinsider.com/koch-brothers-funded-study-proves
   -climate-change-2012-7.
4. https://wattsupwiththat.com/2011/03/06/briggs-on-berkeleys-best-plus-my
   -thoughts-from-my-visit-there/.
5. http://www.wsj.com/articles/SB1000142405274870466260457620277075
   7822548.
6. Ibid.
7. http://www.kochfacts.com/kf/statement-richardmuller/.
8. http://www.nytimes.com/2012/07/30/opinion/the-conversion-of-a-climate
   -change-skeptic.html.
9. https://wattsupwiththat.com/2011/11/17/why-best-will-not-settle-the
   -climate-debate/.
10. Conversation with Muller.
11. https://twitter.com/realdonaldtrump/status/265895292191248385?lang=en.
12. http://www.wired.com/2015/01/senators-dont-believe-human-caused
    -climate-change/.
13. http://www.c-span.org/video/?c4529384/sen-jim-inhofe-snowball-senate
    -floor.

Introduction: America's Muller Moment

1. http://www.nytimes.com/1995/01/03/business/outlook-1995-a-lingering
   -unease-despite-strong-growth.html.
2. http://www.nytimes.com/1996/03/24/books/paperback-best-sellers
   -march-24-1996.html.
3. http://www.dallascowboys.com/news/2008/07/26/former-rb-duane-thomas
   -makes-surprising-visit.
4. Predictit.org.

Snake Oil or the Cure?

1. http://www.pollingreport.com/dvsr.htm.
2. http://time.com/4107636/transcript-read-the-full-text-of-the-fourth
   -republican-debate-in-milwaukee/.
3. http://www.politifact.com/truth-o-meter/statements/2012/sep/06/bill
   -clinton/bill-clinton-says-democratic-presidents-top-republ/.
4. Alan S, Blinder and Mark W. Watson, "Presidents and the US Economy:
   An Econometric Explanation," July 2014, https://www.princeton
   .edu/~mwatson/papers/Presidents_Blinder_Watson_July2014.pdf.
5. Calculation based on data from the U.S. Bureau of Labor and Statistics
   and Blinder and Watson, "Presidents and the US Economy."
6. Blinder and Watson, "Presidents and the US Economy."
7. Ibid.
8. Data from the U.S. Bureau of Economic Analysis (accessed June 2, 2016),
   http://www.bea.gov/national/index.htm#gdp.
9. http://www.nytimes.com/2012/10/27/us/politics/bosses-offering-timely
   -advice-how-to-vote.html?_r=0.
10. http://thinkprogress.org/economy/2015/01/05/3607810/ceo-fire-obama
    -raise-wage/.
11. http://www.nytimes.com/2016/01/31/upshot/to-grade-presidents-on-the
    -economy-look-at-policies-not-results.html?rref=upshot.
12. Jonathan Chait, *The Big Con: Crackpot Economics and the Fleecing of
    America* (New York: Mariner Books, 2008), 13–16.
13. Ibid., 3–20.
14. http://taxfoundation.org/sites/default/files/docs/fed_individual_rate
    _history_nominal.pdf.
15. http://www.heritage.org/research/commentary/2015/7/reagans-tax-cutting
    -legacy.
16. Chait, *The Big Con*, 35–38, 90.
17. http://www.businessinsider.com/about-that-time-the-heritage-foundation
    -said-the-bush-tax-cuts-would-pay-off-the-natioanl-debt-by-2010-2012-11.
18. https://www.youtube.com/watch?v=PtXdPOUMJCk.
19. http://www.dailykos.com/story/2015/6/7/1391360/-Obama-has-created
    -six-times-as-many-jobs-as-Bush.

20. http://www.nytimes.com/2015/08/09/magazine/the-kansas-experiment
    .html.
21. http://www2.ljworld.com/news/2012/jun/19/brownback-gets-heat-real
    -live-experiment-comment-t/.
22. http://www.kansas.com/opinion/opn-columns-blogs/article1096336
    .html#storylink=cpy.
23. http://www.kansascity.com/opinion/opn-columns-blogs/yael-t-abouhalkah
    /article56042540.html.
24. http://krugman.blogs.nytimes.com/2015/05/31/this-age-of-derp-kansas
    -edition/; http://www.kansascity.com/opinion/opn-columns-blogs/yael
    -t-abouhalkah/article56042540.html.
25. http://www.ajc.com/weblogs/jay-bookman/2014/jul/16/kansas
    -conservative-dream-proves-nightmare/.
26. http://www.nytimes.com/2015/08/09/magazine/the-kansas-experiment
    .html?_r=0.
27. http://www.pbs.org/newshour/bb/whats-matter-kansas-unprecedented
    -political-races-leave-republican-candidates-peril/.
28. https://www.washingtonpost.com/business/economy/arthur-laffer-has-a
    -neverending-supply-of-supply-side-plans-for-gop/2015/04/09/04c61440
    -dec1-11e4-a1b8-2ed88bc190d2_story.html.
29. http://www.people-press.org/2014/06/26/the-political-typology-beyond
    -red-vs-blue/.
30. http://www.vox.com/2016/3/8/11178872/donald-trump-policies.
31. http://voices.washingtonpost.com/postpartisan/2010/09/why_obama
    _wont_use_the_word_st.html.
32. Michael Grunwald, *The New New Deal: The Hidden Story of Change in the
    Obama Era* (New York: Simon & Schuster, 2013), 30.
33. http://www.speaker.gov/press-release/five-years-later-where-are-jobs.
34. Grunwald, *The New New Deal,* 376.
35. http://www.cbpp.org/research/economy/the-financial-crisis-lessons-for-the
    -next-one.
36. http://www.fhwa.dot.gov/publications/publicroads/11julaug/05.cfm.
37. Grunwald, *The New New Deal,* 329–35.
38. http://www.cbpp.org/blog/blinder-and-zandi-policy-responses-to-great
    -recession-a-resounding-success.
39. https://fraser.stlouisfed.org/docs/meltzer/maremp93.pdf.
40. http://krugman.blogs.nytimes.com/2015/08/25/unnatural-obsessions/.
41. http://blogs.wsj.com/economics/2010/11/15/open-letter-to-ben-bernanke/.
42. http://thinkprogress.org/politics/2011/08/15/296552/perry-on-bernanke
    -pretty-ugly-down-in-texas/.
43. http://www.cbsnews.com/news/the-end-of-qe2-did-it-work-what-will
    -happen-next/.
44. Grunwald, *The New New Deal,* 377–78.
45. http://www.nytimes.com/2012/02/29/business/economy/republicans

-malign-a-stimulus-but-the-plausible-options-were-few-economic-scene
.html.

46. Grunwald, *The New New Deal,* 413–14.

47. "House Passes GOP Welfare Reform Bill; 'Contract with America' Pledge Sails Through on a 234–199 Near-Party-Line Vote," *Chicago Tribune,* Mar. 24, 1995.

48. http://fivethirtyeight.com/features/elections-podcast-racism-among -trumps-supporters/.

49. http://budget.house.gov/uploadedfiles/expanding_opportunity_in _america.pdf.

50. http://www.wsj.com/articles/paul-ryan-to-propose-sweeping-consolidation -in-anti-poverty-pitch-1406164077.

51. http://budget.house.gov/uploadedfiles/expanding_opportunity_in _america.pdf.

52. http://www.cbpp.org/research/policy-basics-an-introduction-to-tanf.

53. Ibid.

54. http://www.cbpp.org/sites/default/files/atoms/files/tanf_trends_la.pdf.

55. http://www.cbpp.org/research/family-income-support/how-states-use -federal-and-state-funds-under-the-tanf-block-grant.

56. http://www.alaskapublic.org/2016/01/08/leaked-documents-point-to -misallocation-of-federal-funds-at-tribal-group/.

57. http://www.theroot.com/articles/culture/2016/02/when_states_run _welfare_black_children_are_the_ones_who_get_hurt.html.

58. http://www.motherjones.com/politics/2009/01/brave-new-welfare.

59. http://www.c-span.org/video/?c4527266/aei-house-budget-chair-paul-ryan -opportunity-grant.

60. http://aepp.oxfordjournals.org/content/early/2015/06/20/aepp.ppv017 .abstract.

61. http://microeconomicinsights.org/impoverished-children-access-food -stamps-become-healthier-wealthier-adults/.

62. http://www.npr.org/sections/codeswitch/2013/08/26/215761377/a-history -of-snake-oil-salesmen.

63. http://blogs.abcnews.com/thenote/2011/07/newt-gingrich-this-is-the -obama-depression.html.

64. http://crywolfproject.org/quotes/quote-%E2%80%93-rep-newt-gingrich -r-ga-gop-press-conference.

65. The U.S. Bureau of labor Statistics (2016), Labor Force Statistics from the Current Population Survey; http://data.bls.gov/timeseries /LNS14000000.

66. http://www.kansas.com/news/politics-government/article1105569.html.

67. http://www.cbpp.org/blog/blinder-and-zandi-policy-responses-to-great -recession-a-resounding-success http://www.ontheissues.org/2012/Mitt _Romney_Tax_Reform.htm

68. https://www.buzzfeed.com/andrewkaczynski/trump-one-day-into-iraq

-invasion-it-looks-like-a-tremendous?utm_term=.inEwV9qZDq#
.xujeRBb8vb.

69. http://www.foxnews.com/transcript/2015/07/12/mcconnell-webb-jindal
-express-uncertainty-over-iran-nuclear-deal/.
70. http://www.nola.com/opinions/index.ssf/2015/06/bobby_jindals
_disgraceful_fisc.html.
71. http://nymag.com/daily/intelligencer/2016/03/gop-must-answer-for-what
-it-did-to-kansas.html.

America Isn't What It Used to Be

1. http://www.pewresearch.org/fact-tank/2014/10/09/for-most-workers-real
-wages-have-barely-budged-for-decades/.
2. http://www.nybooks.com/articles/2014/05/08/thomas-piketty-new-gilded
-age/.
3. James Carville, *We're Right, They're Wrong: A Handbook for Spirited Progressives* (New York: Random House, 1996), 78.
4. Ibid., 81.
5. https://eml.berkeley.edu/~saez/saez-UStopincomes-2013.pdf.
6. http://www.oecd.org/social/inequality.htm; and OECD (2016), *How's
Life?: Measuring Well-Being*, 89.
7. https://www.whitehouse.gov/the-press-office/2013/12/04/remarks
-president-economic-mobility.
8. Thomas Piketty, *Capital in the Twenty-First Century* (Cambridge, Mass:
The Belknap Press of Harvard University Press, 2014).
9. Robert J. Samuelson, "The Nadir of His Presidency," *The Washington Post*,
December 21, 1994.
10. http://www.pewresearch.org/fact-tank/2013/12/05/u-s-income-inequality
-on-rise-for-decades-is-now-highest-since-1928/.
11. http://www.billoreilly.com/b/Bill-OReilly:-Will-Violent-Class-Warfare
-Break-Out-in-the-USA/347975645374760219.html.
12. http://insider.foxnews.com/2015/06/05/oreilly-income-inequality-play
-giant-ruse-designed-get-votes-dems.
13. George F. Will, "The Great Redistributor," *The Washington Post*, April 23,
1995.
14. https://www.washingtonpost.com/opinions/how-income-inequality
-benefits-everybody/2015/03/25/1122ee02-d255-11e4-a62f-ee745911a4ff
_story.html.
15. http://www.washingtonpost.com/wp-dyn/content/article/2007/01/31
/AR2007013100879.html.
16. George W. Bush, Remarks at Federal Hall, January 31, 2007, New York,
NY; http://www.c-span.org/video/?196488-1/us-economy.
17. https://www.washingtonpost.com/news/wonk/wp/2013/01/02/the-legacy
-of-the-bush-tax-cuts-in-four-charts/.

18. http://www.taxpolicycenter.org/publications/analysis-donald-trumps-tax
    -plan/full.
19. http://fivethirtyeight.com/features/the-mythology-of-trumps-working
    -class-support/.
20. http://www.thedailybeast.com/articles/2015/07/11/trump-in-phoenix
    -mexicans-are-coming-to-take-your-jobs-and-kill-you.html.
21. http://www.pewresearch.org/fact-tank/2015/11/19/5-facts-about-illegal
    -immigration-in-the-u-s/.
22. http://cis.org/sites/cis.org/files/borjas-economics.pdf, 11.
23. http://www.nber.org/papers/w12497.pdf.
24. http://www.foxnews.com/on-air/your-world-cavuto/transcript/donald
    -trump-welcomes-trade-war-china.
25. https://www.uschamber.com/issue-brief/assessing-the-record-america-s
    -trade-agreements.
26. http://nfap.com/wp-content/uploads/2016/05/Impact-of-the-Trump
    -Tariffs.NFAP-Policy-Brief.May-20161.pdf.
27. Piketty, *Capital in the Twenty-First Century*; see also http://www.nybooks
    .com/articles/2014/05/08/thomas-piketty-new-gilded-age/.
28. https://www.hillaryclinton.com/issues/plan-raise-american-incomes/.

Shit Sandwiches

1. https://www.washingtonpost.com/posttv/politics/sen-tillis-maybe
   -restaurants-shouldnt-make-employees-wash-their-hands/2015/02/03
   /4b655ef0-abd7-11e4-8876-460b1144cbc1_video.html.
2. Ibid.
3. http://www.wvgazettemail.com/news/20160308/agency-investigates
   -lawmaker-who-distributed-raw-milk-to-celebrate-bill-passage.
4. http://www.chicagobusiness.com/article/20150220/NEWS02/150229995
   /a-look-at-dire-obamacare-predictions-that-havent-panned-out.
5. http://thinkprogress.org/health/2015/03/09/3631281/obamacare-economy
   -predictions/.
6. Ibid.
7. http://www.politifact.com/truth-o-meter/statements/2016/jan/29/ted-cruz
   /ted-cruzs-pants-fire-claim-health-care-law-nations/.
8. https://twitter.com/GrahamBlog/status/430772731953823744?ref_src
   =twsrc%5Etfw.
9. https://newrepublic.com/article/114991/obamacare-quotes-12-craziest
   -things-ever-said-about-it.
10. Ibid.
11. http://www.cbsnews.com/news/grassley-warns-of-government-pulling-plug
    -on-grandma/.

12. https://newrepublic.com/article/114991/obamacare-quotes-12-craziest -things-ever-said-about-it.

13. Ibid.

14. Ibid.

15. http://www.fool.com/investing/general/2016/03/19/fact-or-fiction -obamacare-is-a-job-killer.aspx.

16. http://www.nytimes.com/2016/02/08/opinion/the-time-loop-party .html?_r=0.

17. http://www.forbes.com/sites/rickungar/2014/02/04/cbo-says-obamacare -will-reduce-employment-by-2-5-million-but-not-for-the-reason-you -think/#464a72a76460.

18. http://www.c-span.org/video/?c4484067/douglas-elmendorf -testimony-aca.

19. http://obamacarefacts.com/sign-ups/obamacare-enrollment-numbers/.

20. http://www.wsj.com/articles/number-of-uninsured-in-u-s-drops-below-10 -for-first-time-in-2015-1463501948.

21. http://nymag.com/daily/intelligencer/2015/12/sorry-conservatives -obamacare-is-still-working.html.

22. http://money.cnn.com/2015/01/21/investing/unitedhealth-earnings -obamacare/.

23. http://www.consumerreports.org/cro/news/2014/08/are-obamacare -premiums-skyrocketing-in-2015/index.htm.

24. http://www.nytimes.com/2016/03/14/us/politics/obama-often-depends-on -mail-to-tell-his-story.html?_r=0.

25. https://www.whitehouse.gov/blog/2016/03/03/brents-letter-president-you -saved-my-life.

26. https://www.propublica.org/article/seven-of-the-most-striking-ways-states -have-loosened-gun-laws.

27. http://www.cnn.com/2015/10/09/us/texas-campus-carry-law/.

28. http://www.usnews.com/news/articles/2016-03-24/petition-allow-open -carry-of-guns-at-republican-national-convention.

29. http://www.nbcnews.com/politics/2016-election/ted-cruz-tout-second -amendment-support-iowa-gun-range-n474431.

30. https://www.washingtonpost.com/news/post-politics/wp/2015/11/14 /donald-trump-says-tough-gun-control-laws-in-paris-contributed-to -tragedy/.

31. http://time.com/4069415/ben-carson-defends-holocaust-guns/.

32. Peter Schroeder, "GOP Chairman: Banks Are Facing Regulatory Water-boarding," *The Hill*, March 15, 2016.

33. Ibid.

34. http://financialservices.house.gov/uploadedfiles/financialservices -doddfrank-report.pdf.

35. https://www.washingtonpost.com/news/business/wp/2016/03/07/why
    -146200-is-a-terrible-bonus-for-wall-street/; http://www.wsj.com
    /articles/u-s-banking-industry-profits-racing-to-near-record-levels
    -1407773976.
36. Data from the "Google Finance" database: https://www.google.com
    /finance.
37. http://www.wsj.com/articles/dodd-franks-effect-on-small-banks-is-muted
    -1443993212.
38. http://www.wsj.com/articles/dodd-frank-creators-on-wall-street-reform-five
    -years-later-1437347191.
39. http://science.time.com/2012/12/17/betting-on-hunger-is-financial
    -speculation-to-blame-for-high-food-prices/.
40. http://energy.gov/eere/vehicles/fact-915-march-7-2016-average-historical
    -annual-gasoline-pump-price-1929-2015.
41. http://bigstory.ap.org/article/897dd6f4a5eb4043b5c24bb0ddd7b7ee
    /regulators-5-big-banks-get-failing-grades-crisis-plans.
42. Adam Smith, *An Inquiry into the Nature and Causes of the Wealth of Nations*, page 206.
43. http://nymag.com/daily/intelligencer/2016/02/snyders-aides-knew-flint
    -water-was-unsafe.html; http://www.nytimes.com/2016/01/30/us/flint
    -weighs-scope-of-harm-to-children-caused-by-lead-in-water.html?_r=0.
44. https://www.washingtonpost.com/opinions/michigan-evaded-the-epa-on
    -flint-we-cant-let-that-happen-elsewhere/2016/03/14/9ecfd46c-e9de-11e5
    -a6f3-21ccdbc5f74e_story.html.
45. https://www.theguardian.com/environment/2016/feb/26/republican
    -candidates-donald-trump-eliminate-epa-law-experts.
46. http://www.theatlantic.com/politics/archive/2016/03/the-real-cause-of
    -the-flint-crisis/472305/.
47. http://www.hsph.harvard.edu/news/hsph-in-the-news/clean-power-plan
    -promises-health-benefits/.
48. https://www.jstor.org/stable/1515174?seq=1#page_scan_tab_contents;
    http://www.theatlantic.com/politics/archive/2016/03/the-real-cause-of-the
    -flint-crisis/472305/.
49. http://www.nytimes.com/2008/09/11/washington/11royalty.html.
50. http://www.nrdc.org/energy/gulfspill/files/gulfspill-impacts-summary
    -IP.pdf.
51. Paul Pierson and Jacob S. Hacker, *American Amnesia: How the War on Government Led Us to Forget What Made America Prosper* (New York: Simon & Schuster. 2016), 74.
52. https://www.washingtonpost.com/business/economy/does-government
    -regulation-really-kill-jobs-economists-say-overall-effect-minimal
    /2011/10/19/gIQALRF5IN_story.html.
53. Mass layoff statistics from the U.S .Bureau of Labor and Statistics.

The Anatomy of Bullshit

1. http://www.cdc.gov/vhf/ebola/outbreaks/2014-west-africa/case-counts.html.
2. For a timeline of Ebola cases in the United States, see: http://abcnews.go .com/Health/ebola-america-timeline/story?id=26159719.
3. http://money.cnn.com/2014/10/15/investing/ebola-spooks-wall-street -investors-stocks; http://www.nytimes.com/2014/10/22/business/demand -jumps-for-protective-equipment-as-ebola-cases-spur-hospitals-into-action .html?_r=0.
4. http://www.businessinsider.com/cdc-ebolas-spread-to-the-us-is-inevitable -2014-8; http://www.ajc.com/news/news/study-simulates-likelihood-ebola -spread/nhGRg/.
5. Ibid.
6. http://www.vox.com/2014/10/13/6964633/travel-ban-airport-screening -ebola-outbreak-virus.
7. https://twitter.com/realdonaldtrump/status/495379061972410369.
8. http://theweek.com/articles/442868/did-republicans-overshoot-ebola -panic.
9. https://www.buzzfeed.com/andrewkaczynski/peter-king-slams-doctors-on -ebola-suggests-ebola-went-airbor?utm_term=.rwyyAxAVJ#.ytm6LbL0n.
10. Mr. Kincannon, not surprisingly, has deleted these tweets. However, cover-age of them can be found here: http://pix11.com/2014/10/07 /former-sc-gop-director-ebola-patients-should-be-put-down-immediately/.
11. http://www.nytimes.com/2014/10/28/nyregion/two-governors-shifts-on -ebola-are-criticized-as-politics-not-science.html.
12. http://www.cnn.com/2014/10/26/health/new-jersey-quarantined-nurse/.
13. http://millercenter.org/president/biography/adams-campaigns-and -elections; http://www.cbsnews.com/news/who-says-political-attacks-have -gotten-worse/.
14. http://www.stuffyoushouldknow.com/podcasts/the-satanic-panic-of-the -1980s/.
15. Adam Shah, Jocelyn Fong, and Zachary Pleat, "Beck, Limbaugh Fomenting Fear about H1N1 Vaccine," *Media Matters for America*, October 27, 2009. Accessed May 1, 2016; http://mediamatters.org /research/2009/10/07/beck-limbaugh-fomenting-fear-about-h1n1-vaccine /155480.
16. http://talkingpointsmemo.com/livewire/mark-udall-isil-campaign-ads.
17. http://www.nytimes.com/2014/11/05/us/politics/midterm-elections. html.
18. http://www.c-span.org/video/?322258-1/hearing-us-response-ebola -outbreak.
19. Josh Rogers, "Shaheen, Brown Press Their Cases In Final Debate," New Hampshire Public Radio, October 31, 2016. Accessed May 1, 2016. http://nhpr.org/post/shaheen-brown-press-their-cases-final-debate.

20. http://www.washingtonpost.com/wp-srv/special/world/how-deadly-is-ebola/.
21. https://www.youtube.com/watch?v=Z2KBfynW09I.
22. https://www.theguardian.com/commentisfree/2014/nov/17/stop-calling
   -me-ebola-nurse-kaci-hickox.
23. http://www.nationalreview.com/article/424293/trump-doesnt-represent
   -republicans-vaccine-question-celina-durgin.
24. http://www.politico.com/magazine/story/2015/01/jeb-bush-terri-schiavo
   -114730.
25. http://www.cbsnews.com/news/doctors-in-congress-criticized/.
26. http://www.washingtonpost.com/wp-dyn/articles/A61435-2005Mar23
   .html.
27. http://www.cbsnews.com/news/doctors-in-congress-criticized/.
28. http://www.washingtonpost.com/wp-dyn/content/article/2005/06/16
   /AR2005061600501.html.
29. http://www.politico.com/magazine/story/2015/01/jeb-bush-terri-schiavo
   -114730_full.html#.V1CL2pMrKi4.
30. http://www.washingtonpost.com/wp-dyn/content/article/2005/06/16
   /AR2005061600501.html.
31. http://benghazicommittee.com/benghazi-by-the-numbers/.
32. https://intelligence.house.gov/press-release/statement-chairman-rogers
   -house-intelligence-committees-final-benghazi-report.
33. https://www.washingtonpost.com/blogs/fact-checker/post/issas-absurd
   -claim-that-clintons-signature-means-she-personally-approved-it/2013
   /04/25/58c2f5b4-adf8-11e2-a986-eec837b1888b_blog.html.
34. http://www.nytimes.com/politics/first-draft/2015/09/30/hillary
   -clinton-calls-kevin-mccarthys-remarks-on-benghazi-inquiry-deeply
   -distressing/?_r=0.
35. http://www1.cbn.com/thebrodyfile/archive/2011/03/08/newt-gingrich
   -tells-brody-file-he-felt-compelled-to-seek.
36. http://www.nytimes.com/2016/05/30/opinion/the-ghosts-of-old-sex
   -scandals.html; http://www.washingtonpost.com/wp-srv/politics/special
   /clinton/stories/hyde091798.htm.
37. Bump, Philip. "Dennis Hastert's Stunningly Hypocritical 1998 Speech
   about Impeaching Bill Clinton." *The Washington Post*, April 27, 2016. Accessed May 1, 2016. https://www.washingtonpost.com/news/the-fix
   /wp/2016/04/27/dennis-hasterts-stunningly-hypocritical-1998-speech
   -about-impeaching-bill-clinton/.
38. http://interactives.dallasnews.com/2016/the-silence-of-ken-starr/.

Interlude: Where We Were Wrong

1. http://www.nytimes.com/2016/04/20/business/economy/liberal-biases-too
   -may-block-progress-on-climate-change.html.

Trump's Original Sin

1. http://www.newyorker.com/news/amy-davidson/donald-trump-and-the -central-park-five.
2. http://www.huffingtonpost.com/2011/01/14/donald-trump-rejects-lind_n _809066.html; http://mediamatters.org/research/2011/04/20/fox-news -goes-full-birther/178860.
3. MJ Lee, *Anderson Cooper 360*, transcript. CNN, July 9, 2015. http://www. cnn.com/2015/07/08/politics/donald-trump-illegal-immigrant-workers/.
4. http://talkingpointsmemo.com/livewire/chris-matthews-donald-trump -birther.
5. Remnick, David. "Trump, Birtherism, and Race-Baiting," *The New Yorker*, April 27, 2011. Accessed May 1, 2016. http://www.newyorker.com/news /news-desk/trump-birtherism-and-race-baiting.
6. http://krugman.blogs.nytimes.com/2007/11/10/innocent-mistakes/.
7. http://abcnews.go.com/Politics/donald-trumps-history-raising-birther -questions-president-obama/story?id=33861832.

I'd Sooner Work for Kim Jong-un

1. Eliza Collins, "Trump: I Consult Myself on Foreign Policy," *Politico*, March 3, 2016. Accessed June 23, 2016. http://www.politico.com/ blogs/2016-gop-primary-live-updates-and-results/2016/03/trump-foreign-policy-adviser-220853.
2. http://uk.reuters.com/article/uk-usa-election-trump-foreignpolicy -idUKKCN0W507S.
3. http://www.politico.com/story/2016/03/full-transcript-politicos-glenn -thrush-interviews-michael-hayden-221275.
4. http://www.bloomberg.com/politics/articles/2016-05-12/trump-foreign -policy-spurned-by-veteran-republican-adviser-baker.
5. https://www.washingtonpost.com/blogs/right-turn/wp/2016/04/27/trumps -incoherent-speech-shows-why-hes-unfit-to-be-president/.
6. Allegra Kirkland, "Graham Rips Trump Foreign Policy Talk: Reagan 'Rolling Over In His Grave," *Talking Points Memo*, April 27, 2016. Accessed June 23, 2016. http://talkingpointsmemo.com/livewire/lindsey -graham-slams-trump-foreign-policy-speech.
7. http://www.weeklystandard.com/rubio-i-still-believe-trump-cant-be-trusted-with-americas-nuclear-weapons-codes/article/2002759.
8. http://warontherocks.com/2016/03/open-letter-on-donald-trump-from-gop -national-security-leaders/.

Conclusion: Do Facts Matter Anymore?

1. http://www.politico.com/magazine/story/2016/03/trump-fact-check-errors
   -exaggerations-falsehoods-213730.
2. To see Dr. Muller recount this story, watch https://www.youtube.com
   /watch?v=6ledD81ofy0.

Appendix: A Voter Guide for 2016

1. http://www.huffingtonpost.com/2011/04/29/donald-trump-blacks-lawsuit
   _n_855553.html.

ILLUSTRATION CREDITS

32: Adapted from the graphic "Average Annualized GDP Growth, by Term," in Alan S. Blinder and Mark W. Watson, of Princeton University's Woodrow Wilson School and Department of Economics, "Presidents and the U.S. Economy," July 2014. The original chart can be found on page 43 of the document posted online at https://www.princeton.edu/~mwatson /papers/Presidents_Blinder_Watson_July2014.pdf.

50: Adapted from Steve Clemons, "GOP Presidents Have Been the Worst Contributors to the Federal Debt," TheAtlantic.com, October 27, 2012; http://www.theatlantic.com/politics/archive/2012/10/gop-presidents-have -been-the-worst-contributors-to-the-federal-debt/264193/.

58: Adapted from an infographic published by the Initiative on Global Markets at the University of Chicago's Booth School of Business. Survey data originally posted July 29, 2014; http://www.igmchicago.org/igm -economic-experts-panel/poll-results?SurveyID=SV_5bfARfqluG9VYrP.

68: Adapted from a graph published by the Center on Budget and Policy Priorities (CBPP); http://www.cbpp.org/sites/default/files/atoms/files /tanf_trends_la.pdf. The graph incorporates data from the CBPP, the U.S. Department of Agriculture, and the U.S. Bureau of Labor and Statistics.

89: Adapted from an infographic, based on data from the Pew Research Center, by Alan Smith for FT.com; http://www.ft.com/cms/s/2/98ce14ee -99a6-11e5-95c7-d47aa298f769.html#axzz4BTjJf6Po.

102: Adapted from the Tax Policy Center publication "An Analysis of Donald Trump's Tax Plan," by Jim Nunns, Len Burman, Jeff Rohaly, and Joe Rosenberg, published December 22, 2015. The Tax Policy Center is a collaboration of the Urban Institute and the Brookings Institution. The original chart can be found on page 12 of the document posted online at http://www.taxpolicycenter.org/publications/analysis-donald-trumps-tax -plan/full.

126: Adapted from "Next Steps for Health Reform," a lecture by Jason Furman, Chairman of the Council of Economic Advisors, at the Hamilton Project, October 7, 2015. The original graph can be found on page 2 of the document posted online at https://www.whitehouse.gov/sites/default /files/page/files/20151007_next_steps_health_care_reform.pdf. Graph is based on data from the "CIA analysis of National Health Interview Survey, Cohen et al. (2009), Klemm (2000), and CMS (2009), and Gallup-Healthways Well-Being Index.

150: Based on data in Jacob S. Hacker and Paul Pierson, *American Amnesia: How the War on Government Led Us to Forget What Made America Prosper* (New York: Simon & Schuster, 2016), 47.

168: Adapted from the Mediamatters.org graphic "Ebola Segments on Evening Cable News." Viewership data covers three networks—CNN, Fox News, and MSNBC—for the dates October 7–November 17, 2014. The original chart can be found online at http://mediamatters.org/research/2014/11/19 /report-ebola-coverage-on-tv-news-plummeted-afte/201619.

ABOUT THE AUTHOR

James Carville is an American political consultant, commentator, educator, actor, attorney, media personality, and prominent liberal pundit. He rose to prominence after spearheading Bill Clinton's successful 1992 bid for the presidency. Carville was cohost of CNN's *Crossfire* until its final broadcast in June 2005. Since 2009, he has taught political science at Tulane University in New Orleans. He is married to the Republican political consultant Mary Matalin, and they have two daughters.